"Small keys unlock large doo[r]... kids' hearts. I've watched Mike Berry live the message of this book. It's doubly inspiring—first, because of what he's done in his own family, and second, because of what his example means for the rest of us. If you're looking to establish a life-long connection with your kids, Mike Berry deserves your full attention."

Michael Hyatt, bestselling author of *Your Best Year Ever* and host of the *Lead to Win* podcast

"Mike captures much of the essence and beauty of parenting, which can only come from years of experience, trial and error, and learning to see our children as God sees us. A must-have for parents who truly want to connect with their kids."

Stephen Arterburn, bestselling author, counselor, pastor, and founder and host of *New Life Live*

"Mike's insight as a parent and a leader in the church will help every parent understand the significance of their role at every phase of a kid's life. *Winning the Heart of Your Child* is a great starting place to understand your role as a parent, shift your perspective, and fight for what matters most in parenting."

Reggie Joiner, founder and CEO of Orange and coauthor of the Phase parenting series

"Add *Winning the Heart of Your Child* to your parenting library today, and your children will thank you tomorrow. Mike Berry's mission to help you win your child's heart will have you laughing, reflecting, and taking action. An important must-read for parents everywhere."

Skip Prichard, CEO of OCLC, Inc., leadership blogger, and bestselling author of *The Book of Mistakes: 9 Secrets to Creating a Successful Future*

"A must-read for all who long to be the best parent or grandparent possible. With humility and authenticity, Mike Berry shares prerequisites for deepening relationships with kids and grandkids no matter what their stages in life. How I wish I would have had such a book as a young mom, but even as a mom of adult daughters and a grandparent, I can still incorporate the life-transforming truths articulated here."

Sherrie Eldridge, author of *20 Things Adopted Kids Wish Their Adoptive Parents Knew*

"This is a must-read for all parents. Drop the guilt and shame and constant worrying about whether you're doing everything wrong in raising your children. Step into smart parenting strategies that actually work, building relationships to last a lifetime."

Cherie Lowe, author of *Your Money, Your Marriage: The Secrets to Smart Finance, Spicy Romance, and Their Intimate Connection* and founder of QueenofFree.net

"Whirling together needed honesty and witty humor, Mike has given us a gift in *Winning the Heart of Your Child*. His invaluable perspective as a parent who understands trauma gives insight into children from a multitude of backgrounds; this book is a must-read for any parent. *Winning the Heart of Your Child* has a perfect mix of self-analysis, loving boundaries, and healthy expectations for all of us. Do yourself and your kids a favor and get this book into your hands."

Natalie Brenner, author of *This Undeserved Life* and writer at www.NatalieBrennerWrites.com

"Mike Berry, from his life experience, understands many things about parenting. At the top of his list is that in order to influence a child, a parent must be connected to their heart. He also understands that parental influence can be hampered by disconnected parenting. This very insightful and practical book introduces parents to the nine keys that open the door to lasting, meaningful, and healing relationships. I recommend this book for any parent who desires to build loving, connected families for a lifetime."

Jayne Schooler, coauthor of *Wounded Children, Healing Homes* and *Telling the Truth to Your Adopted or Foster Child*

"Mike's honesty is refreshing! As a mom through birth, foster care, and adoption, this book reminds me I'm not alone. Not only does Mike share from his personal experiences, but he also gives practical help while extending grace and inspires readers to think long term. As seasons change and your kids grow older, this book is one you will come back to time and time again."

Jami Kaeb, founder and executive director of the Forgotten Initiative

"Mike Berry offers a gift to the world of parenting in *Winning the Heart of Your Child*. The book is drawn from a deep well of personal parenting experience, and Mike encourages, challenges, and supports parents with grace, humor, and realism as they navigate the tumultuous waters of the adolescent and teenage years. This is a must-have for those of us who want to capture the hearts of our children and be an effective influence in their lives."

Jason Johnson, speaker, blogger, and author of *ReFraming Foster Care: Filtering Your Foster Parenting Journey through the Lens of the Gospel*

"As a mom just wading into the tween parenting phase, I'm so grateful to have this book in preparation for the teenage years. While it's a great resource for parents of teens who need a different approach, what a gift it is to those of us who are just setting our course! Many times, I found myself closing the pages of this book and being immediately faced with a real-life 'parenting pop quiz.' I was grateful for the perspective shift and Mike's wise and hopeful voice cheerleading me on. *Winning the Heart of Your Child* gives hope for a better way!"

Jamie C. Finn, author of *Foster the Family*

WINNING
THE HEART
OF YOUR
CHILD

WINNING THE HEART OF YOUR CHILD

9 KEYS TO BUILDING A POSITIVE LIFELONG
RELATIONSHIP WITH YOUR KIDS

MIKE BERRY

BakerBooks

a division of Baker Publishing Group
Grand Rapids, Michigan

© 2019 by Mike Berry

Published by Baker Books
a division of Baker Publishing Group
PO Box 6287, Grand Rapids, MI 49516-6287
www.bakerbooks.com

Printed in the United States of America

Library of Congress Cataloging-in-Publication Data
Names: Berry, Mike (Parenting blogger) author.
Title: Winning the heart of your child : 9 keys to building a positive lifelong relationship with your kids / Mike Berry.
Description: Grand Rapids, MI : Baker Publishing Group, [2019] | Includes bibliographical references and index.
Identifiers: LCCN 2018029376 | ISBN 9780801093692 (pbk. : alk. paper)
Subjects: LCSH: Parenting. | Parent and child. | Adoptive parents. |Interpersonal relations.
Classification: LCC HQ755.85 .B4786 2019 | DDC 306.874—dc23
LC record available at https://lccn.loc.gov/2018029376

Scripture quotations are from the *Holy Bible*, New Living Translation, copyright © 1996, 2004, 2007, 2013, 2015 by Tyndale House Foundation. Used by permission of Tyndale House Publishers, Inc., Carol Stream, Illinois 60188. All rights reserved.

Published in association with Jim Hart of the Hartline Literary Agency, LLC.

19 20 21 22 23 24 25   7 6 5 4 3 2 1

To Rachel, Krystal, Noelle, Jaala, Andre,
Elisha, Jacob, and Samuel.

You've given me the amazing gift
of fatherhood, and I'm forever grateful for it.
I love you each deeply with all that I am.

Contents

Contents

Acknowledgments

I have been a full-time author for three years now, and in that time I've realized just how many people it takes to put a book together. I have so many people to thank I could fill up an entire book alone.

To begin, I want to thank Chad Allen. This book wouldn't exist without you, my friend. Thank you for believing in me and my voice. Thanks for giving me a shot. I'm forever grateful.

Thanks also to Brian Smith. You challenged and stretched me, even when at times I didn't like it. But I'm a better writer for it, and I thank you deeply.

Jim Hart, out of all the many emails that literary agents receive, you chose to read and respond to mine. And you did so right before you were about to head out the door for a family cruise. A million thanks to you for that!

Chad Cannon, your mentorship, insight, and friendship have molded me and shaped me. I'm living my dream thanks to you.

Michael Hyatt, Megan Hyatt Miller, Mandi Rivieccio, and Brandon Triola, your help and generosity have led me to this moment. I could never thank the four of you enough for the gift you gave us several years ago that keeps giving to the world! This book also exists because of your influence.

Jeff Goins, the mere fact that you chose to answer a random email from me all those years ago was one of the greatest gifts I have ever been given. And then you opened the Tribe Conference stage to me in 2016 to share my story. That was beyond kind. I cherish your friendship and belief in me. You are world class, my friend!

Jason and Alison Morriss, Kristin and I cherish your friendship and camaraderie more than you know. We need another ramble in Austin, Texas! Let's get that on the calendar!

Andrew and Michele Schneidler, we owe most of where we are today in our careers to your belief and trust in us. Your friendship and the many laughs we've shared are priceless.

Andrew and Jason, thanks for the many text threads and late-night talks that have kept me sane! Our partnership is so valuable.

My Road Trip brothers from all over the country, I've learned so much from all of you. I love you dearly. Here's to more hikes up the mountain to see the sunrise.

My Refresh family—David, Carrie, Allen, Angelina, Millie, Jyoti, Jenn, and Josh—my deepest love and gratitude. You make this journey fun!

My CAFO family—Jedd, Elizabeth, and Amy—your support has meant everything!

David Enge and Mike Gallagher, I still can't believe you chose to give to and support the work we do before you ever really knew us. Wow! I love you both dearly. I wrote a big chunk of this book at your house, Mike, in Kona, Hawaii, while looking out at the beautiful Pacific. I smile every time I read that section. You both are some of the most generous human beings I know. Thank you!

Peter and Krista Baughn and Jesse and Andrea DeBoer, you have been some of our biggest cheerleaders and supporters, and we are overwhelmed with joy when we think of how our friendship began and how it has grown over the years. This book is for the four of you! You have our hearts forever.

Tony Wolf, my fellow bald and beautiful man! You changed my life five years ago when I had just been fired from my "real" job and you told me you didn't feel sorry for me because I had been given a clean slate to do what I was born to do. You were right! Thank you, thank you, thank you!

My amazing team at Oasis and Confessions—Michelle, Jen, Jeff, Beaver, and Karen—you are the best in the land, and I am eternally grateful that I get to work with you every day! Thank you for believing in our mission and working tirelessly to make sure parents all around the globe are loved and cared for!

Matt McCarrick, where do I even begin with you? Words won't do it justice. What a crazy, amazing journey we've been on since 2001! Thank you for your support and partnership. Most of all, thanks for your continued friendship! We're just getting started, man!

Nate Kreger, your insight, expertise, and belief in our work have helped us to speak hope into millions of parents worldwide. We literally wouldn't be where we are without you. I am grateful for your hard work and friendship!

Darren Cooper, thanks for the great conversations and the friendship over the years. The best is yet to come for you, my friend!

Jackie Bledsoe, thanks for your invaluable advice many years ago that literally became a game changer for our platform. It even helped me complete this project. I'm grateful for you, my friend!

John, Nicole, Ryan, and Megan, you are my forever brothers and sisters, and I couldn't imagine doing this life without the four of you or your precious kiddos. You keep us sane, upright, motivated, and alive most days. You've stood behind us with every crazy, harebrained idea we've come up with and never once have shaken your heads in disbelief. Kristin and I love you all more than you can imagine. And John and Ryan, here's to many more deep life conversations, Marvel movies at Flix Brewhouse, and road trips to see U2. You are my brothers and best friends!

Mom and Dad, thank you for always letting me be me, even when it was confusing or weird. You literally made me who I am. Dana, thanks for loving me even when I was not the best big brother. Love you and Peter for all time!

My second mother and father, Bob and Jenifer Schultz, thanks for being the best in-laws a guy could ask for. Your generosity and belief in both Kristin and me are true gifts, and I'm thankful for you. To my other brothers and sisters— Rebecca, Josh, Rob, Derek, Ali, and Jenny—you mean the world to me, and I am grateful to have you in my life.

The amazing team of editors at Baker Publishing Group, I am simply overwhelmed by your generosity and your belief in this book and this nobody author from the sticks in Ohio. Thank you all so much!

Betty McKinney, my high school journalism teacher, who has left this life. I know you can see this work and you smile. Thank you for never giving up on me and never taking any of my nonsense when I was in your class. Your influence shaped who I am and what I do today.

And finally, to my precious wife, Kristin, who has stood by me through many good times and bad for more than twenty years now. You are the most amazing human being I know. You are filled with unending grace, compassion, creativity, and love. Thank you for never giving up on me. And to my beautiful, amazing, hilarious, and precious kids and grandkids, Rachel (with my son-in-law, Rich, and grandson, Thomas), Krystal (with her fiancé, Tyler, and my grandchildren, Layla and Liam), Noelle, Jaala, Andre, Elisha, Jacob, and Samuel, you fill my heart with light and gratitude every day. Without you, I would be nothing. Thank you from the bottom of my heart! Love, Dad.

Introduction

From My Heart to Yours, So We Can Win Theirs

Ten years.

I used to think ten years was a long time. When I was ten years old, I thought it would be an eternity until I saw twenty. When I turned twenty, it seemed forever till I would turn thirty. Then I turned thirty. . . . You get the idea.

Now that I'm forty-one, I no longer believe ten years is a long time. Correction: I *know* it's not a long time. The other day my wife, Kristin, and I realized that we will be empty nesters in just eleven years. Eleven years! That's not long. Yesterday I was buying diapers for my newborn. Today I'm shopping for her first car. Seems like tomorrow Kristin and I will be moving into a condo, our empty nest.

I've been at this for some time now. We are the parents of eight children, all of whom came to us through adoption. For nine years we were also foster parents of twenty-three children ranging from newborn to high school age. Not only have I experienced my own sixteen-year parenting journey, currently raising children who have been in our care from a young age, but I've also coached hundreds of thousands of parents as a family life pastor and now a family consultant and public speaker. Kristin and I cofounded a blog with over a hundred thousand readers a month in multiple countries. In hundreds of conversations, no parent has told me they wish time would speed up. They all want it to slow down. Or they wish they could regain some of it.

I'm discovering every day how fast time moves. I often feel like I've woken up four quarters into a football game and suddenly find myself at the two-minute warning in this whole parenting thing. This begs the question, What am I going to do with the time I have left with my children?

In 2002, my first child was born. I spent the first few weeks in utter shock—mostly because we adopted her, and the entire process from start to finish took less than three months. There was no initial doctor's appointment confirming the pregnancy seven or eight months before the due date. No ultrasound pictures to share with family. No eight-month gestation journey for mental and physical preparation—redoing a room in our house, shopping for baby clothes, celebrating with a shower. This was airdrop parenting at its best. As I think back on it today, I am beyond grateful. But back then I was clueless. Not just new-parent clueless; time clueless! I thought I had plenty of it.

I was in my midtwenties, three years into my gig as a youth pastor. Kristin and I had been married less than two years, and until our daughter was born we both worked full-time. I worked at a church that demanded much from me. As a young guy, eager to prove myself, I filled up the youth calendar with as many activities as I could. I didn't want anyone to think I wasn't doing my job, so I convinced myself I had to do whatever was asked of me, no matter how often it took me away from my young wife and, soon, my newborn daughter.

I worked at a suburban church that had recently built a new building in a growing upscale neighborhood, poised to become even bigger. So you can bet I worked my tail off. Youth conference? *Added to the calendar.* Retreat? *Added.* Student leadership team? *Also added.* I added and added until my only open night was Saturday. Even my so-called day off was usually filled. I thought I was supposed to do this. More importantly, I thought that since my daughter was a newborn, she needed me less than she would when older. (I also mistakenly thought the same about my wife.)

It's now sixteen years later, and this morning I dropped off that newborn for the start of her sophomore year in high school. She got out of my car, saw her friends, and ran to hug them, forgetting about me. She meant nothing by it. She's a kid. Yet she's also a young woman. "Where has the time gone?" I whisper as I watch her bound across the lot. My heart aches a little, and I snap a quick picture of her with my phone. Then she's gone.

Ahh, time, slow down please, I beg silently. *You are hurting my heart every time I think how fast you are fleeting.*

I pen the pages of this book from a place of wishing I could go back in time and whisper truth to my younger self. It's a place of understanding what it really means to be a parent—how critical it is to understand parental influence and how to lead and love your children to the best of your ability. This is also a plea from me to you: please understand that time goes by faster than you think. Before you know it, that newborn, that toddler, that second grader is beginning her sophomore year of high school, and you suddenly find yourself in the eleventh hour.

The Journey Ahead

Through these pages, I will attempt to help you understand a few key truths. In part 1, I will explain some ways I believe we have gotten our entire approach to parenting wrong. In part 2, I will present nine keys you must understand and apply if you are going to win the heart of your child. These are musts if you want to achieve the healthiest relationship possible with your children, especially during their adolescent years and eventually when they are adults. And in part 3, I will explore what a lifelong relationship with your child looks like, where it begins, and how you sustain it.

In this book, I'm going to take you deep into the interworking parts of a parent-child relationship and show you how to improve the way you interact with and parent your kids. Woven throughout are three central parenting principles:

1. *Understand your influence.* You are the most powerful voice in your child's life. Some of you may have trouble believing this. Trust me though. Your child listens to you, studies you, and believes you. Sometimes this may not seem true when other voices seem louder than yours, but you hold a place of special influence with your child. The key is to use it the right way.

2. *Shift your perspective on your role as a parent.* Believe it or not, your primary role is *not* to teach. Notice I said your *primary* role. Teaching is still a role, but not the first and foremost one.

3. *Fight for what matters most.* As we discuss the nine keys to building a positive lifelong relationship with your child, you'll begin to see how healthily wielding your influence (principle one) and accepting your God-given role (principle two) enable you to win your child's heart.

Hope for All Parents

I write this book to two types of parents. First, I'm writing to the parent of a preteen or a junior high or high school student. You think your child isn't listening to a single word you say. I know you because I am you, and I've been you many times in the past. My hope is that through these pages you will gain a fresh perspective on your influence over your child and on how to encourage the best possible relationship with them. May you come to understand that your voice is crucial during this season of your son's or daughter's life. May you learn to exercise your influence in a new and special way with your child, and may doing so help you reap dividends worth more than gold. May you regear yourself so that you no longer fight merely to win an argument or to enforce your perspective but rather to win your child's heart.

Second, I'm writing to the parent of a newborn, toddler, preschooler, or young elementary school child. You may believe you have a ton of time, so you are not really paying attention to the opportunities you have with your child. My prayer is that this book will prepare you for what is to come and will help you to decide now what is worth fighting for—that is, connection and relationship both now and well into the future. May you be reminded that time waits for no one and is moving at the speed of light. Don't be discouraged. My goal is not to alarm you but to give you a healthy warning. I want to help you accomplish two things—make the most of your time with your child and better use your parental influence.

Are you ready to get started? Me too!

Here's to healthy parental influence. And here's to fighting for what matters most—the heart of your child!

PART 1

THE GREAT
MISUNDERSTANDING

1

Winning the Argument but Losing the Heart

Pick the Right Fight

"Sometimes it is easy to forget that you can win the argument and force the right behavior but lose the heart in the process."[1]

This statement by Carey Nieuwhof, from the book *Parenting Beyond Your Capacity* by Reggie Joiner and Nieuwhof, hit me like the proverbial ton of bricks. I was sitting in a local coffee shop, reading under a single overhead light on a chilly Indiana morning, and watching patrons move quickly in and out of the shop, grabbing coffee and pastries on their way to work. I instantly replayed the previous night's argument with my then eleven-year-old daughter. My words echoed in my mind—every syllable that I had thought at the time was making a pretty darn good point, every dominating fact that shut her down and put her in her place while elevating me as the genius all-knowing, all-seeing father with whom she should instantly agree with zero argument. I had spent many years thinking an argument victory was making a lasting impression on my children. But that morning I was convicted. For the first time, I saw the great canyon I was forging between my children and me.

I could identify with Nieuwhof's explanation of the inner dynamic that drove him to win: "Like a lot of dads, I get wound up when my authority is challenged. It's in me as a man to go head-to-head and fight to win the argument, to crush the rebellion, and to prove that I am in charge."[2] Yep, that was me. After all, that's the way I was raised. That's how my mother and father dealt with my disagreement, my rebellion, my crossing their boundaries.

Even as I type these words I cringe. I missed the point so miserably. I can still see my little girl standing dumbfounded as I dominated the conversation, interrupting her, refusing to let her speak, driving a massive wedge between her heart and mine. She had come to expect this from both my wife and me, to the point that she began to go silent.

There I was the next morning, feeling guilty as I read, "You can win the argument . . . but lose the heart." That's exactly what was happening every time my daughter upset us or disagreed with us. God has given each child a voice, but we were quick to silence hers. We only cared about proving her wrong and winning what we thought most important—the argument. We had lost sight of what was indeed most important—*her heart*. Her spirit was fragile, learning and growing, and we couldn't see that we were crushing it by dominating every conversation.

Circumstances from her past also speak to her reaction. We had adopted her a few years earlier when she was three.

Before that she had spent time in two foster homes. She had come from a place of trauma, so it was no surprise she struggled at first to see us as her parents. She had learned to shut down in heated situations—her defense mechanism—so she struggled to articulate her thoughts and feelings. From among her options—fight, flight, or freeze—she chose freeze. This made it easy for two highly driven firstborns, who didn't come from trauma, to prove our points and win arguments. But that was wrong. We were clueless about what we were doing to our daughter.

Thus my regret, my guilt, and my shame at what I had done. I sat alone, sipping coffee, wiping tears, in sudden realization of what I had been doing to my child through my insatiable need to always be right. If she had had a cell phone at the time, I would have flooded it with a dozen texts, apologizing. I was tempted to drive the thirty minutes to her school, pull her out of class, and hug her.

Why Must We Always Win?

It's hard to blame any of us who have fallen into the trap of thinking we must always be right in arguments or other interactions with our kids. As you read this, you may be feeling the same guilt or shame I felt. You may realize that you've fallen into the same trap of constantly fighting to win, proving your child wrong, and working to elicit a response that indicates you are getting through. Don't beat yourself up. Parenting is hard work, and we spend much of our time trying to figure out just how to relate to our children. Then we blink, and they have entered a new season. Everything we thought we knew we have to adjust or relearn, especially with teenagers and particularly with difficult ones. Plus, many of us grew up in an era when discipline was swift and the rod was never spared. Or we had parents who lectured. (That was my wife's and my childhood story.) So it's understandable that we approach parenting with the methods that are familiar to us. We lecture, we instruct, we teach, and we allow no negotiation. Our parents used this approach on us, and it worked (mostly). But there is a better way.

Here's the thing. We don't always have to win the argument. Do you realize that always "winning" risks losing your child's heart? If we must always be right, always prove our point, always have our way and allow no room to hear our children's voices, we create a new danger. We leave no margin for their hearts to grow and flourish. What's more, we teach them they have no voice, no say in life.

When I was growing up, my dad was often angry and always had to have the last word. This taught me two things. First, I needed vigilantly to watch everything I did or said because at any moment I could cause a blowup. Most of my childhood was spent tiptoeing around to avoid waking the bear. My sister and I would watch the clock every day, knowing the exact moment Dad was due home. We had to be sure our toys were picked up. Nothing—and I mean nothing—could be out of place. Any disorder would prompt a lecture or rant or belittling tirade. Even when everything was in order, we might still face a dressing-down. What a terrible thing for children to go through, but that was our life.

Second, Dad's conquer-all attitude taught me to keep my mouth shut. It was better to stay quiet and wait until the lecture ended. Or if I spoke, to simply agree. My dad had to have the last word, so what was the point? As a result, I carried an inability to speak up for myself well into adulthood. I also struggled with major insecurity and a sense of inadequacy. Even now, in my forties, I wrestle with this from time to time. My dad had won every argument, but he had lost my heart. It wasn't until well into my adult years that we repaired our relationship. We have a good one today, but for many years we did not.

At every age—whether elementary, preteen, junior high, or high school—our children have fragile hearts. Make no mistake about this. Yes, they are resilient, but their ability to recover has its limit. With so much on the line, we lose much by our insatiable need to win. Our children do need boundaries (which we'll talk about later), and structure is good. In no way does winning the heart (rather than always winning the argument) mean that our children can say or do whatever they want. There is a time and a place for discipline, especially when a child's choices are unwise. But we must pay closer attention to the *why* behind the argument and the true ultimate stakes.

Choose Your Win

In this book, I want to make a case for a different approach—a paradigm shift—to parenting. After seventeen years as a parent, eighteen years coaching numerous parents, and now writing and speaking to hundreds of thousands of parents around the United States, this new approach is what I believe is the healthiest means to eventually (key word, *eventually*) enjoying a lifelong relationship with our children.

When we focus solely on winning the argument, we may with good intention be giving priority to our parenting role

31

as teachers. As I've explained, we must be teachers, but we must give even higher priority to our other roles, such as being listeners and defenders of our children's hearts. Successful, positive parenting is not built merely on external behavior modification. Nothing authentic ever is. It's built on a fierce focus on the heart, communicating in such a way that our children know above anything else that they are valued, loved, and cherished.

I would love to go back in time and change those moments when I got it wrong with my daughter. But all I can do is change my interactions going forward. Even more important is changing my *intentions*. She needs a mom and dad who cherish her. She needs a father who, no matter the circumstances, lets her know how much she's valued, even if she has disappointed us with an unwise choice.

Just recently, our daughter did something that warranted a consequence. She made a decision that was not only bad but also unsafe. In the past, Kristin and I would have gone in loaded for bear. We would have anticipated her arrival home from school like a hunter waiting in the shadows for prey. That may sound overdramatic, but sadly it's close to the truth. Fortunately, we talked over lunch that day and agreed on a wiser approach: "When she gets home, we'll sit her down and affirm that we love her. We'll state precisely the problem with her poor decision, outline the consequence, and be done with it. No extended explanation or lecture." And though we told her we loved her, we also went on demonstrating our love in action. Why so short and simple? Her heart is more important than a win in the argument column. Our old method of parenting was dangerous.

Unhealthy methods may modify our children's outward behavior but at what cost? What are we losing by coming out victorious? Too much, if you ask me. I believe in a way that positively influences our children at every age and wins their hearts in the process. It comes down to our tone, attitude, and intention.

That chilly morning as I read *Parenting Beyond Your Capacity* and was cut to the heart, I realized for the first time how critical my words are to my children. That's when I began to change.

Perhaps this is a beginning for you too. Maybe after reading this chapter you are feeling convicted, as I was. That's okay. I couldn't change the past, and neither can you. But you can change your present and future. Try to let go of regret and shame, and view your parenting journey through the lenses of hope and new resolve. Change starts here, and this change can transform your parenting forever.

Pause to Reflect

1. What was the priority for your parents—winning arguments with you or winning your heart?

2. Which of these has been your past priority with your children?

3. What is one new way you can emphasize your love for your child and your child's value?

4. What will this require you to *stop* doing or to do less often?

2

Boundaries Built with Love

One Essential for Parenting Influence

She collapsed on the sofa in my office like a building with a crumbling foundation. Tears welled up and she sniffled, staring at the ground. Her husband sighed, took off his coat, and sat next to her, grasping her hand tightly.

"It's okay," I said gently. I rocked in my plush, black office chair, watching the two closely.

For what felt like an hour, no one said a word. I knew why they had called. I was their last hope, the final thread before their rope snapped and they gave up altogether. They had tried our church counseling department, their school guidance counselor, and even a few out-of-pocket therapists. They were desperate, lost, inching ever closer to complete hopelessness.

Nothing was getting through to their son. Through elementary and middle school, he had earned all As. His teachers had raved about his work ethic, willingness to help others, concern for his fellow students, and good nature. Then all that changed. His grades plummeted. He became cold and closed off and would do nothing to help his younger sister. He was apathetic toward everything and totally disconnected from his parents. He was a month shy of his sixteenth birthday, and the couple feared what he might do once a driver's license came within his grasp.

Every day after school was the same: get off the bus, say nothing in response to his mom's cheerful greeting, insert iPhone earbuds, and drown out the world. He behaved this way for weeks on end.

When they could get him to join family activities, he soon withdrew or became negative. I asked whether he had expressed thoughts of suicide or self-harm, but they assured me he had not.

Finally, the reservoir holding his mom's tears broke, and streams raced down her cheeks. She laid her head on her husband's shoulder, beyond distraught. I handed him the Kleenex. He held her close and reassured her.

Then she said something I've heard hundreds of times: "What happened to my baby? He's changed! He's not the same little boy I remember. I feel as though I'm losing him."

At that point I knew the time was right to gently help them gain a new perspective. I said, "Tell me about your son's younger years, when he was five, six, or seven. How did you parent him back then?"

They looked knowingly at each other. She said hesitantly, "We never told him no because we were afraid that would ruin him. I hated it when he was upset about anything. I never wanted him to suffer. So I built a Bubble Wrap world around him. I know doing so was wrong. But I didn't know what else to do."

"And now that he's a teenager? What do you do now when he crosses a boundary?"

"Fight!" the father blurted. "We fight all the time. We can't get him to do one thing we say. To gain control, we've taken away almost everything, every freedom. I hate to admit it, but I tend to lecture when I feel I'm not getting through. But he just shuts down. What a waste!"

I appreciated their honesty, and through several meetings I helped them peel back every layer of their parenting history. They came to understand the mental shifts they had missed at each stage, which would have guided their son toward security and healthy responsibility.

But they saw no hope of ever having a positive, healthy relationship with their child. When I spoke of their influence and how it's as real and present as it had ever been through the adolescent years, they furiously shook their heads in disagreement. They couldn't believe they had even an ounce of influence in their child's life. But they did; they were just looking for it in the wrong way. They were walking the same road as millions of other parents.

Your influence on your children may be hard to recognize, especially during the teen years, but when you understand and maximize it (by the nine keys I'll explain in part 2), you'll build a brighter future for both them and you. If your kids are younger, there is good news. You don't have to end up in the same difficulties as many parents. You can make a different outcome more likely. This book's concepts won't prevent or solve all problems because we're human beings dealing with little human beings. Your children will push your boundaries in their journeys to discover who they are.

They will mess up. But I'm going to challenge you to respond with new methods to win their hearts.

For those of you in the middle of the preteen, junior high, or high school years, don't lose hope. You can formulate a plan and rechart your course, even though it may seem late in the game. No matter who you are, what mistakes you've made, or how distant you feel from your children, you can win their hearts.

Two Critical Errors

Most parents begin with a desire to raise healthy, happy children of character and virtue. I've never met a parent who, when holding their newborn, thought, *Gosh, I hope I screw this kid up!* Yet many enter the journey unaware of a few critical principles, and they end up in despair and frustration.

The parents in the story I just shared suffered from two critical errors. Their first error was that, because of their own upbringing with harsh rules, they were reluctant to set healthy boundaries for their son for fear he would hate them. But boundaries don't have to be harsh restrictions. Later they overreacted when their son stepped out of line. Instead of targeting the heart, they aimed to win the argument. Their idea of influence was offtrack. They struggled with leading their child in a healthy way, and their response was to become dictators. They teetered between trying to be his buddy and being sergeants at arms when things went south.

I can understand parents who shy away from setting boundaries and guidelines, especially a new parent who fears the words *no* and *stop*. Those who grew up in households full of strict rules that made little sense are prone to lax boundaries for their children.

But the reality is that a lack of boundaries is harmful for our children. Healthy discipline equals love. In Proverbs 13, King Solomon wrote, "Those who spare the rod of discipline hate their children. Those who love their children care enough to discipline them" (v. 24). Solomon used strong words: not disciplining our children means we hate them! In this context the word *hate* doesn't mean a deep-seated, evil hatred. Rather, it means that sparing discipline is falling short of complete love for our children. Think about the importance of boundaries in our lives. When boundaries are absent, chaos ensues. It's that simple. If my wife and I didn't set boundaries, our children probably would tear off drywall and set the house on fire. I'm kidding, but there's some truth in it. We need boundaries to survive and function properly in this world.

Think about a lack of boundaries in terms of our society. What if there were no laws or structure? What if government ceased to exist? What if no law enforcement officials maintained civil order? What if we were permitted to do whatever we wanted, whenever we wanted? We would be stuck in a terrifying situation.

The second critical error the parents in my example made was to harshly enforce the boundaries they had established (assuming they had communicated the boundaries clearly, which many parents don't). Oftentimes, parents resort to a commander or instructor mentality (which we'll discuss in the next chapter). This happens because parents fear losing control of their child if they aren't strict. It also happens because the parent is looking for a response in the face of passive aggression. For years I struggled with this very thing with my oldest son. He was defiant and belligerent and needed to be reminded of the boundaries we had set. He also needed to be reminded (repeatedly) not to disrespect others, including his parents. I feared losing control of him, so I turned up the harshness. His response was a passive-aggressive refusal to acknowledge me, which frustrated me, and I became even harsher. My strict approach eventually garnered the reaction I wanted and I maintained control (or so I thought), but I missed out on a connection with my child.

When I finally stopped trying to ensure his "proper" response through harshness and once I began to state my expectations without lecturing, my son began to respond in a far more positive manner. If you are shaking your head because you've struggled with this, you're not alone. Let me encourage you to hang in here with me. In the chapters ahead, we'll discuss healthy and positive parenting methods in greater detail.

Loving Boundaries

We all—including our children—need boundaries. But here's the big question: Do boundaries and discipline need to be harsh? Not at all.

If sparing "the rod of discipline" means falling short of full love for our children, what does the rod refer to? Is it lecturing or scorning or belittling? No. The rod is a principle. And principles are important and meant to be paid attention to. You could actually replace the word *rod* with the word *principle*. In other words, King Solomon is telling us that if we spare the principle (or critical action) of discipline, we're falling short of loving our children. Even the word *discipline* is up for interpretation. Nowhere in human history does healthy discipline equal dictatorship. Discipline doesn't mean you lecture until you've won the argument or proven your point. Can you enact boundaries and discipline in a calm, collected, loving manner? Absolutely. In fact, winning our children's hearts in love *requires* that we set boundaries and take an uncommon approach when our children cross those boundaries.

I like to compare healthy boundaries to guardrails, which are normally placed a distance from the danger zone. Wise parents establish boundaries that teach children to stay a safe distance from danger. I think of an especially dangerous stretch of highway near my hometown in central Indiana—perhaps the most dangerous stretch in the United States. There are always backups, accidents, and lots of tailgating. I recommend you avoid this stretch at all costs. Unfortunately, I used to travel it quite frequently. Once while sitting at a standstill in traffic, I noticed a lake-sized retention pond beside the highway. It had jagged edges from excavation, and it was deep. Driving into it would be certain death. But between the road and the lake was a sturdy guardrail. Beyond that were fifteen to twenty feet of grass and then a row of trees. Before anyone could get close to the lake, they would have to make it over that stout guardrail, across the grass, and through the trees. I have seen many cars smashed into the guardrail, but I've never seen any in the grass or near the lake—thanks to a guardrail placed a safe distance from the danger zone.

Guardrails don't provide as much safety if they are built right at the edge of the danger zone. Toppling over a guardrail built at a cliff's edge results in a headfirst plummet to annihilation. For parents, this analogy simply means lovingly establishing boundaries well before your child nears danger. If you want your child to have respect for the opposite sex, to refrain from sex outside marriage, and not to drink before age twenty-one, set and discuss boundaries during the preteen or junior high years, not when they are already well into high school. The night of senior prom is too late.

Healthy boundaries are most effective when they are established in love. Again, many of us think of boundaries as harsh or negative, often because we were raised with harshness, lectures, shaming, or scorn. You may need to change your perspective on what loving boundaries really look like.

Loving boundaries should begin when children are toddlers. Setting healthy boundaries could have kept many parents from having to come see me over the years, distraught over their out-of-control teenagers after years without boundaries.

Loving boundaries are conversational at first. We have a rule in our household that no one wears shoes past our mudroom. We live on a farm in central Indiana where winters are particularly gross. Our backyard and driveway are basically mud pits from October through April. We talked about this when we first moved in, and we talked again when we noticed muddy footprints in the kitchen. We grew more stern the third time. And finally, when we had to repeat ourselves a fourth time, we handed down a consequence. Even then, we did not threaten, shame, or lecture. We calmly, firmly communicated the boundary and outlined the consequence. Of course, tracking mud through our home isn't a serious danger, although it is irritating. But you get the idea. Even a boundary talk about sex or curfew or touching a hot stove can be conversational. It might involve *tough love* (a term we'll discuss later, which may carry a negative connotation for some but does not involve meanness, harshness, or shame), but it can still be a calm conversation.

42

What can you do now? We'll discuss these principles in greater detail later, but to get you started, here are a few immediate action steps:

1. *Start now.* Don't make the mistake of thinking you are too late. Or too early. Whether your child is two, six, or a teenager, start now. If your child is older and you've been lax on boundaries, you may have a greater challenge, but your child will benefit even by your late, appropriate efforts.

2. *Explain what you are doing and why.* I recommend a sit-down conversation, especially with your tween, junior higher, or high schooler, before setting and enforcing boundaries. The conversation should include what the specific boundaries are, the consequences for crossing them, and why you are doing this. And you need to make clear in word and deed that your love is unwavering, even if your child thinks you are being cruel.

3. *Set and enforce boundaries.* This seems obvious, but I want to spur you on to actually *do* this. Reading, talking, or thinking about boundaries doesn't set them. Be proactive. To start, select a limited number of boundaries in areas that are especially important or where you are more likely to establish a pattern of success.

4. *Be consistent.* When you set a boundary but are lax about enforcement, you send a message to your child that this boundary isn't really important. Consistent enforcement of your communicated expectations helps your child take you seriously. And eventually they will come to understand the value of your boundaries.

Pause to Reflect

1. What parenting ideals has your upbringing created in you regarding boundaries, discipline, and influence?

2. How have you struggled with establishing and maintaining healthy boundaries for your children?

3. What are your biggest fears in parenting?

4. What do you choose to believe about your influence as your children's parent?

5. If you could accomplish one thing in raising your children, what would that be?

3

What the Gilmore Girls, Buddy the Elf, General Patton, and Mr. Strickland Share in Common

How Not to Parent Your Child

A few years ago, the internet was in complete meltdown. At least that's what it looked like from my vantage point as my teenage daughters danced excitedly around the house. It was announced that Lorelai and Rory Gilmore and the entire Stars Hollow gang would be reuniting for a special Netflix-only series called *Gilmore Girls: A Year in the Life.* Our household would consume no other television outside this series. My wife and two daughters made sure. I had no choice but to join them.

Okay, I'm kind of a fan too. I loved the original series years ago, often watching during lunch breaks with Kristin and my second-oldest daughter. But before watching the new series, we decided to go back and watch the originals from the get-go, when Rory was but a wee, witty school kid who prompted laughter and wonder. Some of the best television writing I've heard.

I noticed something interesting as we watched the original series together—Lorelai was, by every measure, a passive parent. She was young when Rory was born, so her relationship with her daughter was more friend-to-friend than parent-to-child. Their tense interactions and even major conflicts seemed to get ironed out perfectly (in the span of one to two episodes). This is not necessarily a bad thing. For Lorelai and Rory, it seemed to work. But something interesting often happened when young Rory would goof up—Lorelai would lose it. In several episodes, they fought. So a friend-to-friend relationship would work until Rory screwed up.

Around the time we binge-watched the new series, we also consumed another familiar family classic—the Christmas movie *Elf*, which the Berry household continues to enjoy year-round. I think that DVD spent six months in my Suburban's player. Driving one day, while my sons watched *Elf* for the thousandth time, I began to think about the character depictions of Lorelai and Rory Gilmore and Buddy the elf. Lorelai and Rory have this beautiful, witty, high-spirited relationship. Even their conflicts are short-lived and resolved within an episode or two. Only once did they remain at odds for half a season. Some might see theirs as the near-perfect mother-daughter relationship and fantasize about living it.

Comparing ourselves with fictional characters may seem silly to some. But in many ways, the Gilmores are our fantasy family, right? Let's go back to the hospital or adoption agency for a moment. How many of us held the following mental picture of the way we hoped this parenting gig would go? We will raise our kids with love, and they will rise and call us blessed every morning. We won't fight, and they will hang on our every word. Our conversations will be deep and always end in complete agreement. They will be good students and athletes, well liked by others, and well adjusted. They will hold our views on everything from the economy to politics to sports.

This sounds idealistic. But we think like this, don't we? I call it the Dreamer parenting approach—the idealized version of parenting most of us envisioned at the outset.

Then there's Buddy the elf. He loves everyone. He's everyone's friend, even if friendship is not the best option. He likes smiling. He doesn't want anyone to be mad at him or unhappy in any way, so he's eager to please. He wants to be with you all the time and do whatever you want to do.

Many of us are like this, willing to go to any lengths to make our children happy. Let's call this the BFF (best friends forever) parenting approach. No matter what the child's choices or attitudes toward parents, the parents are determined to be their child's friend forever. Throughout my nearly two decades working with families and coaching parents, I've seen this approach used many times.

In 2005, I was serving as youth pastor in a small church in central Indiana. I loved that job. We experienced some great years there with many fond memories. But I remember a particular family with kids in our elementary, junior high, and high school ministries. Their family was highly active in the church, and their children attended every event we hosted, always the first to sign up. The parents were the first to open their home for a youth event or to volunteer as sponsors for a trip. They were highly committed, but they were also very lax with their children. Not that the kids were bad—they were kids. The older two were "blessed" with wild spirits. The parents often laughed off the kids' boundary offenses. They fit the Buddy the elf approach to a T. They never wanted to say no to their children. It was as if they idealized their children, refusing to believe they were capable of making bad choices and needed boundaries.

On one youth trip, one of their kids became involved in a conflict. What seemed to be innocent teenage behavior turned into a big ordeal and upset several other students. After piecing everything together, I had to inform the parents. They refused to believe their child could have done what other students and adults claimed. Even when other trip sponsors explained the severity of the situation, they failed to discipline their child and establish healthy boundaries to keep their child a safe distance from danger. Later they said, "We don't want our children to hate us. We have an understanding and close friendships with our kids. We don't want to mess that up." I couldn't believe what I was hearing.

These parents knew many parents who ruled like military generals, resulting in broken relationships with their teens. I could understand because in some regards I grew up like that myself. But I've also known many overly permissive parents. I've counseled some over the years, and I've seen the harm that comes from the BFF approach. Still, these parents had a point. They were describing a third parenting approach—the General Patton approach, or the Commander.

The fourth parenting approach is closely related to the Commander. I call it the Instructor. Some parents turn everything into a lecture and a lesson, though unlike the Commander, the Instructor may be very kind.

Okay, Mike, I'm tracking with you. But I have to disagree on a few things. First, I have a good relationship with my kids. They respect me, and I respect them. I would even consider them friends. So I don't think there are dangers in the Gilmore Girls or Buddy the elf types of parenting.

I think it's great that you have a congenial (and hopefully healthy) relationship with your children. I really didn't say you didn't. And I love that you are friends. I'm not saying that the Lorelai or Buddy parenting styles are entirely bad. They have some merit.

But whether your children comply or push boundaries, at some point they will need you to establish and enforce healthy boundaries. They need you to show them the way, to guide them, and to teach them how to be adults in this world. Even the best of kids pushes a boundary here or there. (Any kid who never tests a boundary is probably unhealthily compliant and may end up rebelling somehow later in life. They may do this either passive-aggressively through subtly warped adult dysfunction or overtly with employers, friends, family, or even complete strangers.)

Let's take a closer look at these four parenting styles.

The Dreamer Approach

Lorelai Gilmore appears to have a perfect peer-to-peer relationship with her daughter, Rory. This type of parent-to-child relationship definitely exists, especially in your *future* relationships with your children. But when entering parenthood, idealized expectations can be dangerous. Countless parents have admitted this error to me. They invested fully in the hope of something that wasn't realistic. As their children

49

grew older, the parents fought hard to protect their vision. But this view of their relationship with their children, the hopes they had built up in their minds, even the expectations they had, screeched to an abrupt halt when their children entered the preteen and teen years. They experienced mourning and regret and struggled to cope with the new normal. And they spent a small fortune on Kleenex.

In meeting with these parents, the toughest thing I had to do was walk them through, step by step, year by year, the many instances when their fantasy clouded their view of a healthy parent-child relationship. The fantasy spawned denial of what was actually happening in their home.

We don't want to fail but to succeed as parents. But Dreamers misunderstand how parenting success is really defined. Parenting success is not a problem-free journey with our children. It's expecting problems and dealing with them in responsible, sometimes painful ways. It's refusing to believe the fantasy and seeing instead the reality of our kids' wonderful, imperfect hearts. As we will see in later chapters, the imperfect truth about our children is far more meaningful and beautiful than any "perfect" dream.

The BFF Approach

The BFF approach to parenting is closely related to the Dreamer approach. The BFF style simply says, "I'm your buddy no matter what!" It stays friendly regardless of the child's attitude, words, and behavior. All parental effort goes into trying to please them.

In the movie *Elf*, one scene captures this perfectly. Buddy the elf shows up as Michael, his half brother, leaves school at the end of the day. Buddy waves, calls out, excitedly follows, and persists in talking nonstop. But Michael abruptly tells him to go away and leave him alone. Buddy doesn't clue in and keeps following. Michael grows more annoyed and verbally offensive. It's clear that Buddy will stop at nothing to be Michael's friend, no matter how rudely Michael responds.

I've seen this approach unfold in numerous families. I've been berated by parents who couldn't understand why my youth staff and I would discipline their child for bullying another kid at summer camp. They explained, "That's what teenage boys do!" I've witnessed parents enabling their child's addictive behavior because they feared the child would hate them or rebel if they no longer allowed a computer in the child's bedroom. A 2016 study conducted by the Barna Group in partnership with Josh McDowell Ministries reported that 27 percent of young adults between twenty-five and thirty first viewed pornography before puberty, in part because parents put few or no restrictions on web-browsing devices. Roughly 16 percent of kids say they come across porn daily, 32 percent weekly, and 23 percent monthly. Thirty-three percent of women between thirteen and twenty-four seek out porn at least once a month. Pornography is a problem for boys *and* girls, and a major gateway is through smartphones.[1]

This is precisely why we have one computer in our house, and it's in the most public place. Our teenagers do not have social media or internet access on their iPhones, and they have to charge them in our room at night, no questions asked. I'm not their buddy; I'm their father. My making them happy pales in comparison with keeping them safe and instilling them with character, integrity, and a moral compass.

Attempting to be our child's buddy at all times neglects the child's need for a life model. They are not likely to take us seriously as a source of advice and guidance into adulthood. There is space for friendship in some ways, but clear, healthy, and enforced boundaries teach kids how to be adults. Last year on our podcast, we were discussing influence, and my wife said, "We're not raising children; we're raising adults!"[2]

Another reason the BFF approach is dangerous is because it sets unrealistic expectations for our children. In the real world, their authority figures aren't likely to be their buddies. While our children are under our roof, we have the opportunity to model what they should expect of a realistically healthy authority figure, loving our kids even as we exercise discipline.

The Commander Approach

Often parents misunderstand the dangers in overcontrol or fail to realize they have fallen into it, especially if they grew up with a parent who used this approach. A Commander goes beyond strict; General Patton is about control, command, and zero negotiation and often uses shaming ("What's wrong with you?" or "How could you?"), belittling ("What kind of an idiot . . ." or "You've got no sense"), or rigidity to achieve control.

Strict parents can be influential parents if they provide a healthy blend of love and boundaries, as we saw previously. But while General Patton parents might love the child, they withhold expressions of love that seem "soft." Commanders fail to understand that respect is earned by *showing* respect to their children and by vulnerably seeking forgiveness when they wrong their children.

The 1999 film *The Virgin Suicides* had a huge impact on my view of parenting. It's about five sisters living in the 1970s Detroit suburbs. Their strict Catholic parents, Mr. and Mrs. Lisbon, closely supervise the girls, imposing harsh religious requirements and even isolating them in their home. After their youngest daughter takes her own life, the parents intensify their scrutiny. One of the neighborhood boys, Trip, eventually convinces Mr. Lisbon to allow the girls to attend the homecoming dance, after which the oldest daughter has sex with Trip, falls asleep, misses curfew, and takes a taxi home the next morning. Mr. and Mrs. Lisbon freak out and impose a complete lockdown.

Isolated like caged animals, the girls spiral downward into risk-taking behaviors—sneaking out, sleeping around with boys and grown men—and fall into deep depression. (Spoiler alert!) Under Mr. Lisbon's continued enforcement of the lockdown, the girls eventually all take their own lives through a suicide pact with each other.

As I watched this movie as a twenty-two-year-old college student, my heart was crushed. I couldn't understand how these parents didn't see that their efforts at protecting their children were the very force that pushed them into danger. But I know many Commander parents. Often they've made serious mistakes in their own past, and they reason, "I don't want my children to end up like me." But allowing fear to be their driving motive blinds them to its real effects—pushing their kids away and creating a desperate urge to escape, rebel, or self-harm.

We're going to see that you can be healthily firm with your kids without controlling them. This will lift a lot of weight off your shoulders, and your kids will respond much better to reasonable boundaries and loving enforcement.

The Instructor Approach

I call the Instructor approach the Mr. Strickland approach. It's related to the Commander approach but with stark differences. If you grew up in the eighties (or happen to be an old movie buff like me), you'll remember the movie *Back to the Future*. In the beginning of the film, Marty McFly has some run-ins with his high school principal, Mr. Strickland, who berates and lectures him on his tardiness. This principal is tough, never missing an opportunity to instruct or correct.

Parents who lean toward the Mr. Strickland approach see everything as a lesson or a teaching moment. When their child goes four for five on the softball field, they spend the drive home explaining how they could have made it five for five and had a perfect day. When their child asks a simple question about an algebra problem, they break out the whiteboard and spend the next hour doing equations. Their child's curiosity is squelched in the name of so-called enlightenment. This approach is generally more docile than the Commander, but not always.

The biggest problem with this approach is that the Instructor misses opportunities to connect with the child's heart in authenticity and love. Children ask questions because they love us and look up to us, not because they want a lesson.

Well, Mike, my children happen to love being taught new things.

Really? Have you asked them? Ask if they'd rather listen to an hour-long lecture on solving algebraic equations or get a moment with Mom or Dad solving a problem and connecting hearts? Allow them to answer honestly.

If you are prone to instruct, you may be losing your child's heart. The danger is subtle, and you may not see it until it's too late. But if you catch this tendency now, you can learn to teach your children more through example and loving acceptance and less through lecture.

Pause to Reflect

1. Which parenting approach have you struggled with the most?

2. In what good or bad ways has this struggle affected your relationship with your child?

3. What are three things you want to do differently with your growing child?

4

The Ugly Stepsisters of Parenting

Create a New Parenting Pattern

Kristin and I are both extremely driven individuals—crazy over-the-top-organized-must-happen-no-ifs-ands-or-buts driven! We are also natural lecturers, partly because we grew up being lectured.

My childhood home was very vocal, and arguments quickly escalated to shouting matches. We all yelled nonstop, competing for the last word. More than just lecturing, those yelling matches were freighted with shame and contempt. I regularly heard "What's wrong with you?" or "Are you stupid or something?" or "What kind of idiot does something like this?" My impressionable heart captured the self-image of a fool, a failure.

The way we react to our kids' bad choices sends a message about what we think of them. Our responses to their human struggles stay embedded in them into adulthood. Our hearts may wish to help them, but shaming words will prevent them from seeing our true hearts, and they will never learn to do better.

Not that long ago, one of my kids was caught stealing red-handed. Yes, stealing. The act was caught on camera, and the evidence was literally spilling out of his bedroom. He had stolen candy from three different stores and stuffed the wrappers under his mattress. We were not only angry but also embarrassed, ashamed, and bewildered.

We debated, we discussed, and we wrestled over our next move. We both wanted to shout at him. Our instinct was to lecture, to shame. But we knew none of this would work. Think about a time you were belittled growing up. Did it make you want to do better? My parents' yelling and lecturing had zero effect on me, except that I found new, unhealthy ways to fake it or escape or defend myself.

Children are already on shaky ground. Their hearts—even those of teenagers—are ultra fragile. They are trying to find their way through this overwhelming world, and insecurities fill their minds and hearts. This is especially true of children who've come into a family through adoption. They often believe they are failures because their birth parents chose not to keep them. An inner voice repeats this lie, whispering that they are broken, unfixable, or unwantable. That, my friends, is the voice of trauma.

We believe that our children are beautiful, bright, talented, and perfectly designed, and it's our desire to speak this truth to them above the voice of trauma. But when we shame or lecture, we reinforce what that lying voice tells our kids. This is not the way to teach them to do better.

Shaming and lecturing are the ugly stepsisters of parenting in families parented by Commanders and Instructors.

Families of Dreamers and BFFs also have ugly stepsisters, such as denial, living in fantasy, and disconnection from reality. These are just as harmful in their own ways as yelling, lectures, and put-downs. When we attempt to be the perfect fantasy family, we ignore the real problems and needs that should be addressed. When we try to be our children's buddies, we fail to give them the parental guidance and instructive boundaries they crave. When we parent like Dreamers and BFFs, we build a shaky foundation for our kids, lacking the firm solidity of truth and moral rightness that kids need as their foundation.

What do we do, then? How do we, imperfect adults, parent our imperfect children? I believe the better way involves a paradigm shift and avoids all four of the unhealthy parenting approaches.

Disabuse the Dreamer

As I said, it's easy for parents to fall into the Dreamer approach because we begin this journey with a strong desire to do what's right for our children. While some parents actively harm their children, the Dreamer's problem is passive avoidance of what a parent *needs* to do. We can so desire to live out the perfect parenting picture that we deceive ourselves with a fantasy rather than parent with intentionality.

How can we disabuse the Dreamer?

Real Relationships, Not Pretend Perfection

The Coldplay song "Politik" asks for the real, not the fake.[1] These words have become a life motto for my family. Fake doesn't last. Fake is fleeting. Fake eventually crumbles. Consider how cheap knockoffs cannot stand up to the authentic versions. Or how pretending only lasts until the game is up and someone is exposed. Actors portray "real" life on the set of a movie, but when filming ends they go back to *real* life.

We need real in this world. And we need real in our relationships with our children. I've encountered many Dreamer parents, and I want to scream at them, "The Gilmore Girls aren't real. They are actors!"

We must dial ourselves into reality with our children and stop pretending that we or our families are something we're not. Disabuse the Dreamer by accepting and dealing honestly with the authentic difficulties and complications of real relationships.

Meaningful Messes, Not Counterfeit Order

We live in the age of Pinterest and Instagram, where everyone's lives are chronicled in detail for the world to see. The apparent perfection social media communicates makes spectators feel less adequate by comparison. Just last night, Kristin and I were sitting in our cluttered dining room—filled with unpacked boxes from our recent move—talking about the many parents who portray counterfeit order on social media. They want the world to see how great they are, while the rest of us limp along the parenting journey. But we know the truth—they are not real.

We tried counterfeit several years ago, and it just deepened our longing and loneliness. When we embraced the messiness of our family, our journey became meaningful. Some of our eight adopted children have significant special needs.

Our journey has been different from that of families whose children entered the world biologically. It's been messy. But I wouldn't trade any of it, not for a million different, so-called picture-perfect scenarios. Our life is deeply meaningful because it's adventurous and wild and sometimes risky. The social media accounts I love are the ones that gladly show off the mess. I can relate to them 100 percent.

Balance the BFF

The BFF approach is related to the Dreamer approach. It's dangerous because, like the Dreamer approach, it also passively avoids what a healthy parent needs to do. It defaults to what is comfortable in the moment. Think about your friendships—your relationships with other adults, extended family, or even your spouse. They are founded in part on comfort. We are comfortable with our friends. Friends enrich our lives and make us feel good, as they should. Now and then a friendship hits the rocks and a come-to-Jesus meeting is necessary. But normally having a good buddy around fills us up.

But trying to be best friends with our children is unhealthy because it bypasses the necessity for healthy boundaries and guidance through the formative years. To the degree that the harder aspects of love allow us to have friendships with our children, that's not wrong. We have had opportunities to relate to our children as friends. We'll talk more about this later in the book, but we do take full advantage of conversations and positive interactions with our children. We actively listen to their perspectives on the world around them and to their opinions. We sit in coffee shops with our teenagers and laugh at the crazy stories they tell about the happenings in their school or the ridiculous post someone they know left on Instagram. We sit around our dining room table and joke back and forth during a meal. In a sense, we enjoy a level of friendship with our children at these times. But friendship can't be our guiding principle as parents. We can't sacrifice boundaries and guidance in the name of friendship.

How can we balance the BFF?

Love, Not Buddies

Love takes many forms for parents, even some forms that our children won't like in the moment. The fact is sometimes our kids like us, and there is peace. And other times we have to make decisions they may not like but that are healthy for them. That's love.

You've probably heard the term *tough love*. Perhaps tough love is necessary right now in your parenting. Despite the negative connotation, I wish everyone understood that this is healthy love. Healthy parenting requires love that must sometimes be expressed through enforcement of boundaries and guidelines, even when it would be more comfortable to be a buddy.

Parents, Not Peers

There will be moments when you can relate to your child as a peer, but you are always a parent first. As a youth pastor, I trained adult small group leaders, trip sponsors, and mentors. One of the main principles I taught was that students don't need another buddy; they need a mentor. They don't need another best friend; they need a guide to help them figure out this thing called life. How do they fit in the world?

62

What is their purpose? What are they called to do? They are looking to you, the adult, to help show them the way.

Your role as a parent is the same. Your children do not need another peer, even when that feels easier. They need a parent.

Calm the Commander

Dreamers and BFFs both neglect what parents *should* do. In contrast, the Commander does what parents should *not* do—shame and control.

Again, if this has been you, don't beat yourself up. We as adults have learned to be responsible, and we often project our adult expectations onto our children before taking a step back and considering a healthier way of guiding them.

How can we calm the Commander?

Compassion, Not Contempt

You want to lose your temper. I know; me too. Many times I have. You've gone over something so many times before with your kids. You've laid out the guidelines, clearly outlined the consequences, and enforced the boundaries. Yet here you are again. They've blown it, and you are tempted to scorn, lecture, and shame because these tactics get a reaction. And doesn't that reassure you that you are getting through? Maybe. But at what cost?

I know that my kids came to my wife and me already convinced they were failures—not good enough, unwanted, unworthy of love. Your children too may wrestle with the not-good-enough bug. Our contempt at their mistakes only reinforces this. It's time to adjust our approach and let compassion lead the way. We must still reinforce consequences and allow natural consequences to run their course, but we can do this with compassion rather than scorn or shame.

We teach this topic in parenting classes around the country every year, and almost always someone in the audience asks for examples. The key is to pay attention to your tone and body language when addressing your child. Ask yourself, How does my voice sound right now? How is it making my child feel? What are my actions communicating to them? It's easy to allow your emotions to control your response, prompting harsh words and actions. But you don't have to raise your voice to communicate that your child has done something wrong. In fact, there is great power in remaining calm and collected as you speak with them.

Also, refine your words in both quality and quantity. Emotions can lead us to go on and on when a simple, to-the-point statement will do.

Walking With, Not Walking Over

What if—in spite of our children's mistakes and failures— we were to make the active choice to walk *with* them as they learn rather than walk *over* them to gain compliance? What if we were to *show* them rather than *tell* them? We need to bury the old saying "Do as I say, not as I do." That's an unhealthy parenting style. We must encourage our kids and teach by example, especially when they have made a mistake.

Interrupt the Instructor

Like the Commander, the Instructor actively does what a parent should *not* do. Why isn't lecturing a healthy approach?

Let me remind you how you feel when you've been lectured to and a more relational connection would have been more helpful. You feel awful, belittled, not seen.

Our children want relational connection. They want to know we really see them. They don't want everything they do wrong to result in another lecture from Mom or Dad. Some of my children were adopted from hard places, and they have struggled with identity and believing they matter. If I resort to lecture, turning everything into a lesson, I create distance in the relationships.

How can we interrupt the Instructor?

Observation, Not Just Instruction

We often so heavily emphasize our parental role as Instructor that we lose sight of our children's hearts. We need instead to stop and observe their hearts—ask ourselves questions about who they are and take delight in that—before we try to teach them. How many parents take the time to get to know their children? What do our kids hold valuable? What are their dreams? How do they see the world around them? What are the reasons behind their choices? The reasons for certain behaviors are not always what we think, and we might choose a different response after listening and learning rather than jumping to conclusions. Recently, my sixteen-year-old daughter was in a bit of hot water for something we perceived had happened over one of her social media channels. Kristin and I talked it over and decided what her consequence should be. But when we sat down with her, a battle erupted that lasted a few hours. The more she argued the firmer we became on the consequence. And on it went until something extremely valuable happened. We started listening more closely to what she was saying. We gave her space to explain her perspective, and we actually listened (which can be tough for driven people to do). We discovered that our perception of what had occurred wasn't actually what had happened. And we discovered this by giving her space to explain and actively listening. Please understand me. Discipline is necessary for wrong choices, and it may need to be swift. But take a little extra time to discover what's happening in your kids' hearts and minds, and listen—really listen—before deciding on a consequence.

Intentionally choosing to connect relationally to your child is no passive cop-out. It's actively choosing an approach different from the way you were taught or from what feels good. As my good friend Jason Morriss said, "Choosing not to shame or instruct or correct but rather to stand in observation of our child's brilliance and delight in them and love them with no strings attached is as good as active parenting gets." And I can tell you from personal experience, it's a slam dunk for parents.

Criticizing our children reinforces what they already believe about themselves. They often carry a dark passenger of self-criticism, insecurity, and shame with them. But through observation, taking delight, loving, and showing compassion, we can help lay this dark passenger to rest and build trust and connection in its place.

"I Love You," Not "How Could You?"

Barking "How could you?" or "What were you thinking?" is belittling. Our kids may not know the answer. We have to understand that they probably weren't thinking. Many are impulsive, even well into their twenties, because of the natural developmental process. Or if your kiddos are anything like mine, perhaps the part of their brain responsible for reasoning is damaged or dormant due to trauma. For others, fetal alcohol spectrum disorder has permanently damaged the executive functioning skills in the brain's prefrontal cortex. With any of these causes, we may think our children are lying when in reality their brains are simply incapable of normal adult reasoning. So let's give our kids the benefit of the doubt. When they blow it, let's say "I love you no matter what" and reinforce our words with loving action because actions speak louder than words.

What to Do about Past Mistakes

You may be reeling with regret over past failures with your kids. Listen to me. Stop beating yourself up. You are human. You and I make mistakes, sometimes in abundance. Perhaps you closely identify with the Dreamer, BFF, Commander, or Instructor, and you are guilt ridden. Maybe out of deep emotion or frustration, you've resorted to shaming or lecturing to get a point across to your child. Or maybe you've been too passive or permissive and have missed opportunities to provide firm guidance. Don't give up hope; hang in here with me. We're about to move into the pay dirt. Life is about learning, and by God's grace you can make a new start today. Grace makes everything new, including you!

If none of the four approaches we've discussed leads to long-term, life-guiding relationships with our children, then what approach does? How can we apply both truth and love with our children?

The answer is the Influential parenting approach, which we'll explore next.

Pause to Reflect

Complete one or two of the following exercises based on what best fits your tendencies and parenting style:

1. Dreamers: List several less-than-perfect aspects of your relationship with your child. Choose one and plan how you will accept it and even make use of it for a healthy, *real* relationship, rather than an unrealistic fantasy.

2. BFFs: Plan a conversation with your child. Tell them how much you love them, and explain the importance of your role as a guide and authority in their life.

3. Commanders: Make a list of things you can say to your child to express compassion and acceptance. For example, "That must have hurt your feelings" or "I still love you, and I always will." Review these once a day so that they will come to mind when needed.

4. Instructors: Write down the things you've observed about your child that are brilliant, amazing, hilarious, and beautiful. Write a short note of encouragement telling these things to your child.

PART 2

PARENTING FOR THE WIN

5

Everything I Know about Influence I Learned from My Mother-in-Law

Key 1: Blend Love and Discipline for Influence

My wife and her mom have a great relationship. They talk on the phone almost every day, sometimes for hours, about everything from parenting to church to marriage to current events to politics to cooking to holiday scheduling. Sometimes the laughter or silly bits I overhear make me think Kristin is talking to one of her girlfriends. Then I find out it was her mother. Their transparency used to make me nervous, but I have come to value my mother-in-law as one of our biggest cheerleaders on our journey as parents, former church workers, and now authors and public speakers.

Kristin and her mother are best friends, but it wasn't always this way. Through Kristin's elementary and adolescent years, her mother was not Lorelai Gilmore or Buddy the elf.

But neither was she General Patton nor Mr. Strickland. She was *influential*. She exercised a solid merging of love, guidance, friendship, and discipline. She set solid boundaries and never wavered. She understood that sometimes the strongest love a parent can show is in follow-through and consistency, even when it's excruciating.

My wife is a firstborn child, as am I. We both pushed the boundaries. She describes her young self as "a stubborn, argumentative, hardheaded kid." The other day she told me a story from her high school years: "Mom and I went to lunch and had a great time talking, catching up, and giggling at the awkward boy behind the counter in the sandwich shop. She was like a friend. She always took time for me and my brothers and sisters. She was interested in me, my heart, and who I was.

"But she knew how to be a parent. That same night I went to a home football game. My curfew was 11:00 p.m. sharp. But I came in at 11:25. My mother was waiting for me. She calmly and matter-of-factly said, 'Where were you?' I shrugged, and she continued: 'Your curfew is 11:00 p.m. and you are late.'

"I argued that it was only twenty-five minutes, but she persisted. 'Your curfew is your curfew. You are grounded for the weekend.' That's all she said. She didn't lecture me or scorn me or teach me how a clock works. She said it calmly, and that was it. And she stuck to this punishment. Just because we had had a great time at lunch didn't take away her responsibility as a parent. I screwed up, and she busted me. I carry so much respect for my parents for never backing down from their boundaries."

Whoa. Stop and think about that. I could end this book right now with that paragraph. I could simply say, "Do this!" But you'd send me nasty emails accusing me of cheating you out of the money you paid for this book, so I'll keep going.

My wife went on to explain that, growing up, she had many friends with parents like Lorelai Gilmore, Buddy the elf, General Patton, or Mr. Strickland. Today, more than twenty years later, none of them to her knowledge have a healthy or deep relationship with their parents. She told me the story of a high school friend who was allowed to do anything she wanted. "Man, I was so jealous of her," Kristin said. "She got to stay out late, go to anyone's house, and never got in trouble. I always thought, *It must be nice to be her.* It seemed like a dream."

But it wasn't. Her friend's parents ended up divorced, and the family fell apart. The parents' lack of boundaries was only one part of a larger cluster of problems—a by-product of other issues the mom and dad faced. But Kristin has seen the profound impact of the no-boundaries approach on her friend.

Her friend's parents were uninvolved, disconnected, and misguided on effective parenting. Kristin's parents, in contrast, were influential.

Influential parents know how to seize relational opportunities and how to set clear boundaries and stick to them. They understand that the merging of love, connection to their child, healthy boundaries, and discipline when called for result in maximum influence. Like guardrails, healthy boundaries allow room to deviate but are also set a good distance away from danger. They allow for a bit of give-and-take. Healthy boundaries allow the child to be a free individual while also keeping them safe from danger.

As a youth pastor, I talked with many kids who said things such as "My parents don't care when I come home. They don't care who my friends are. They don't care how late I stay up. They don't care what movies I watch or what websites I visit." Usually these kids were frustrated with their parents for a variety of reasons. But the central statement I heard over and over was "My parents don't care." How far does the love of these parents go? Far enough to take full advantage of the great gift parents have—their influence? Or only far enough to feel warm toward their kids until disaster strikes?

Influential parents care deeply for their children. They are willing to seize the moments they are given to deepen relationships—moments to encourage and build up their children. They also seize moments of responsibility to guide, lead, establish healthy boundaries, and discipline. Kristin's mother lunched and laughed with her daughter and reinforced a boundary in the same day. She wasn't caught up in an idealized version of their relationship that blurred her vision. She wasn't worried Kristin wouldn't like her if she imposed a consequence for a clearly crossed boundary. She enacted a reasonable sentence with calm, firm love.

We all want to be influential parents. But it requires learning to use our influence in the right ways, at the right times, and in love. A healthy balance of love and discipline puts an entirely new light on our relationships with our children and helps ensure the very outcomes many try to achieve through ineffective methods.

This first key is probably the most crucial for a parent to understand. You do have influence as a parent. But how do you make the most of this influence? How do you begin to see yourself as an influential parent?

Believe in Your Influence

Many parents shake their heads when I tell them they have influence with their children, even during the teenage years. They simply don't believe it. Maybe pop culture or childhood experience has implanted itself too deeply in their thinking. But we must believe we have influence. I'm willing to bet you picked up this book because you want to learn how to win your child's heart. You fear all the things in this world that fight for control of their lives and their souls. I get it. I'm there with you. But my challenge to you is that if you don't believe you have influence in your child's life, the rest of this book is meaningless. It begins here. I know "Believe in yourself" is a cliché, but it's still valid. You must believe in what you have been given in order to maximize your relationship with your child.

Think Long Term

You must view your parenting as a long-term investment. I will get into this more in chapter 15, but it's important to note here. A retirement or college savings account does not reach maturity and pay full dividends after only a few years of investing. Neither will you see the final fruit of your parenting influence until many years down the road. Kristin and her mom have a rich, endearing relationship today, but it was formed over a twenty-year period. What you do now—whether your children are young, adolescents, or high schoolers—leaves a lasting impression on the rest of their lives.

Remember Your Why

Several years ago, I had the opportunity to spend a day in Nashville, Tennessee, with virtual mentor and leadership expert Michael Hyatt. During lunch he said, "People lose their way when they lose their why." When we don't know why we are doing something, when we've forgotten our purpose, we get lost. This has never been truer than in our parenting journeys. As a youth pastor, I met with many broken parents, distraught over alienation from their teens. It became clear they had lost their why as parents, and thus they had lost their way. They couldn't remember the passion they once had. Remember that you are in this because you love your child, and ultimately you want to raise a human being who lives with character and integrity and who leaves a lasting impression on the world.

Commit Yourself to the Here and Now

Keep looking and dreaming toward the future, but live in the present. Think long term about your investment, but don't get caught up in fantasizing about "someday." We sometimes think if we can make it through the trying seasons—diapers, taxiing kids around, dealing with back talk—we will reach a golden age of peace and understanding. But we miss so much in the present when we fixate on the future. Every new stage brings a new challenge. When I finally got past having to pack an entire trailer with baby paraphernalia for vacations, I then had to start reminding the kids to clean up their trash in the van. Stay focused on today's stage and where your children are right now.

Pause to Reflect

1. What practical steps can you take to seize your greatest opportunity as a parent—your opportunity to genuinely love and influence your child in a positive, healthy way?

2. Think about the unhealthy parenting approaches described in chapters 3 and 4. To which of these are you most prone? How can you use a healthy merging of love and discipline to change your old approach and win your child's heart?

6

Fourth Place Can Win

Key 2: Understand and Embrace "The Shift"

Throughout the year, I travel around the country, sometimes with Kristin, speaking to parenting groups on adoption and foster care, using parental influence, the spiritual roles parents play, and much more. I love to travel. A recent eight-day trip took me from my hometown of Indianapolis to Seattle, to Denver, to Breckenridge, Colorado, back to Denver, on to Colorado Springs, back again to Denver, and finally home to Indianapolis. *Whew!* That was exhausting just to type.

On my final flight out of Denver, I was ready for home. I was exhausted and coming down with a cold. I pictured walking in the door, my young sons running from the living room and tackling me. I could see my daughters hugging me and hear them saying they missed me. Fortunately, it was night, so none of my fellow passengers could see my goofy smile or my tears. Sure enough, when I walked in the door that evening, I was greeted by my little men and beautiful girls, and the whole scene played out a second time, now in the real world.

Coming home from a long, country-spanning trip is one of my favorite things because of this encounter at the end. If you have young children or had them at one time, you've probably had a similar experience. It's one of a parent's favorite moments. We also love when our children want to hang out with us. Sometimes it can be wearing on us, especially for stay-at-home moms or dads, but mostly it's great. We are our child's world during their early stages of life. Up to age nine or ten, they want to do everything with us. We are who they think about all day at school, and we are who they want to tell everything that happened that day. They come to us with their boo-boos, fears, and frustrations.

Your centrality in your child's life is the reason you are the greatest voice of influence in their life—spiritually, intellectually, and emotionally. Your young children are taking their life cues from you on just about everything. Think about your life now as an adult, and ask yourself, What things do I do now that my mother or father did? I bet you can name a few. That's influence. Some of us enjoy a strong spiritual life because of our parents' influence. Some save money because of their frugal parents. Others imitate their parents' strong work ethic or drive to succeed. You shape much of your child's future character and priorities during their first ten years when they heed your every word and want to be like you. Young children think their parents hang the moon and stars. You are at the top of their ranking of people's influence on them:

1. you
2. other adults
3. friends
4. culture

Close behind parents are other adults—schoolteachers, Little League coaches, Sunday school teachers, next-door neighbors, grandparents, or aunts and uncles. After them are friends—neighborhood friends, classmates. Then comes culture. Our kids love Disney shows and cartoons, but they are not heavily influenced by either. Sure, we will hear a Sponge-Bob SquarePants quote or a line from a movie now and then, but that doesn't reflect significant life-changing influence.

It feels good to be on top, doesn't it? Ranked number one and loving life with your child. But then around age eleven, twelve, or thirteen, a seemingly overnight shift occurs.

Carl E. Pickhardt, in an article titled "Adolescence and the Influence of Parents," explains:

> Parents vastly underestimate how closely they are observed and how constantly they are evaluated by their child. In the vanity of their superior position, parents prefer to think they know the child best, and perhaps this is for the best. Otherwise, being the object of such keen and relentless scrutiny might make parents too self-conscious for their own comfort.
>
> From childhood to adolescence to young adulthood, however, the judgmental thrust of this evaluation tends to change. The child tends to idealize the parents, the adolescent tends to criticize the parents, and the young adult tends to rationalize the parenting received. Here's how it often works.
>
> The child (up to ages 8–9) admires, even worships parents for the capability of what they can do and the power of approval that they possess. The child wants to relate on parental terms, enjoy parental companionship, and imitates the parents wherever possible. The child wants to be like and to be liked by these adults who are mostly positively evaluated (assuming they are not damaging or dangerous

81

to live with). A child identifies with parents because they provide the primary models to follow after and to live up to. So childhood evaluation of parents begins with idealization. At the outset, parents are usually too good to be true, at least for long.[1]

Notice he uses the verbs *idealize, admire, worship*, and *imitate*. If you are parenting a child in this age range, or if you have done so, you probably know this to be true.

The Shift of Influence

At adolescence, the rankings change, taking most parents by surprise. You went to bed one night comfortably ranked number one among your child's influential people, and you woke up the next morning to find everything rearranged:

1. friends   3. other adults
2. culture   4. you

What happened? you wonder, perhaps a little panicked. You may lament to God or a friend; something has changed with your little boy or girl. They no longer greet you at the door. They don't always want to be with you. They are listening to other voices.

This generally happens when a child reaches the preteen, junior high, and high school years. Suddenly their friends are everything to them. You tell your daughter her outfit doesn't match and her shoes will make her uncomfortable. She rolls her eyes and sneers because her friend says the outfit looks *adorable* and those shoes are *to die for*. This happens in every arena—music, movies, culture, slogans (does anyone else hate LOL, IDK, or TTYL?), and just about any aspect of your child's worldview. When The Shift happens, friends hyperjump to the number one spot of influence, and culture suddenly gains much more influence, followed by other adults. Finally, in lowly fourth place, sits you, the parent—the one who brought this defiant, hardheaded human into existence or who chose to welcome the child into your home through foster care or adoption.

Dr. Pickhardt continues: "Now comes adolescence (beginning around ages 9–13) and parents get kicked off the pedestal. In the girl's or boy's childhood they could do no wrong; come adolescence it seems they can do no right. What has caused this sudden fall from grace? Have parents changed? No, but the child has, and with cause."[2]

This is, unfortunately, the season when many parents give up, disengage, or close down. They realize something has changed and conclude there is no point in trying to get their teenager to listen or to care about anything or anyone but themselves. Often in this season, out of desperation, parents escalate to BFF mode—trying to be their child's buddy—or to Commander mode—controlling their child's every move. They may resort to a desperate grasp of the idealized Dreamer's fantasy of the perfect family, mourning the failure of their unrealistic dream. Some transform into Instructors, lecturing in response to their misunderstanding of The Shift. Or they may switch from one strategy to the other when one doesn't work.

Your natural response to finding yourself ranked fourth may be panic, hopelessness, pulling back, or overcontrol, but you'd be missing one glaring truth: *You are still on the list!*

Check it out. There you are—number four. Yes, you've dropped in the rankings, and your child's friends seem much more powerful now. And your child is consumed with a culture that demands allegiance. But you are still on the list of influential voices.

It's easy to throw your hands up at this stage and surrender. It's easy to believe that you've lost any chance of a healthy relationship with your kid, especially if you fight often. Kristin and I have been there several times. In fact, we are currently smack-dab in that trench with you, parenting two teenagers. Through much trial and error—mostly error—we've realized the important truth that I mentioned earlier: *the parent is still the most important voice of influence in a child's life.* That's true whether you agree or not. It's hard to see, but your kids are still taking life cues from you. They seem to be following everything friends or culture tell them, and you often seem to be ignored or blown off, but your children are still quietly listening to you, needing you in their lives. Someday, their ideals will closely resemble yours.

But you are not the *only* voice. You must be willing to recognize and even accept that. Doing so actually benefits you in your parenting, and in the next chapter we'll talk about the wisdom of voluntarily widening your child's circle of influence. But for the moment, let's consider a few things you shouldn't and should do when you reach this season.

The Big Don'ts and Dos When You Are Fourth

It is not impossible to parent through this season. I promise. I've survived, and so have many other parents. In fact, this season is not just about survival. It's about thriving and building the kind of relationship with your teenager in the present that will pay enormous dividends in the future. I'm going to walk you through a proven strategy here in part 2.

When you suddenly wake up and realize The Shift has happened, there are several things you should *not* do:

1. *Don't panic.* I know you want to. I know you are tempted to give in to the knee-jerk feelings, but don't. Remember, this is a season, not necessarily the definition of the rest of your child's life or your relationship with them.

2. *Don't be a Dreamer.* Avoid the trap of fantasy or idealization about your role and your relationship with your child.

3. *Don't try to be your kid's BFF.* Over the past seventeen years, I've counseled more parents than I can remember who resorted to buddying up to their kid, trying to compete with pop culture influence. It doesn't work.

4. *Don't be a Commander.* In your moments of panic, you may become super restrictive and forceful, demanding complete compliance with the rules. While you need to create and maintain healthy boundaries, these can't be the same for a teen as for a younger child. The consequences have to be discussable.

5. *Don't be an Instructor.* It's easy to default to making everything a lesson when you feel you are not getting through. But this risks pushing your child away. There are times for lessons, but you must choose these times wisely. For the most part, say it once, then let it go.

So what *should* you do when The Shift happens? Here are the six critical answers:

1. *Stay the course.* The rule of thumb when you drop from first to fourth place is *steady as she goes.* Keep your hands on the wheel, eyes forward, and stay the course. Don't freak out (or do so only with another adult), and don't resort to the ineffective strategies listed earlier.

2. *Guide, don't just enforce.* You now have an opportunity to guide your teenager, to teach and model a firm, loving, and calm demeanor, leading in love. They might not always want to hear what you have to say, but deep inside they will tuck away those nuggets of advice. Yes, you must set and enforce consequences for crossed boundaries. Discipline when discipline is necessary, but, as always, never harshly.

3. *Give teens space to be themselves.* Remember, teenagers are free-thinking, self-determining human beings. You need to give them space to breathe. Don't become the overbearing parent who tracks their every move. Accept and even encourage your child's discovery of their way. Set boundaries that allow plenty of space for healthy individuality.

4. *Maintain boundaries.* Even though you need to give teens their space, it doesn't mean that boundaries or household rules get thrown out. Disrespect is still not to be tolerated, nor are poor choices. You may need to modify established boundaries to better suit this new season, but it's critical that boundaries remain.

5. *Find supportive community.* I can't encourage this enough. You need to meet regularly with two or three

other parents and dump your truckload of emotions over the whole teenage dramafest. You need to wear your poker face with your kids, so you need a support community as an outlet.

6. *Embrace fourth place.* Learn to be comfortable with fourth place. You really have no choice; it is going to happen. You must allow the circle of influence to grow wider during the teen years. Value and support the small group leader or youth pastor at church, who can speak the same truth you are speaking into your child but with a better outcome. It's tough to hear your teenager respond positively to other adults when they don't want to listen to you, but these other individuals are your God-given allies, and they will benefit you and your kids greatly.

Pause to Reflect

1. How do you react to the idea of The Shift, or to the reality of The Shift if you've already gone through it? What are some constructive alternatives to your natural response?

2. If your child is still pre-Shift, identify one or two ways you can prepare for it.

3. What has hindered or might hinder you from staying the course with your child? How can you counter this?

4. In what ways could you benefit from the support of other parents? Who will they be?

7

You Need a Bigger Circle

Key 3: Amplify Other Voices of Influence

I used to lead groups of high school students to a weeklong summer conference in Michigan, the highest-attended student conference our church offered. Its impact on students' lives was everlasting. Every June, we loaded a bus with energetic students who were expecting spiritual transformation and to gain a fresh perspective on their lives. Upon their return, they were always ready to turn the world upside down, "on fire for Jesus!" as we used to say. Their hearts were filled with love, compassion, and focus on their peers.

Even more valuable were the relationships that developed between students and adult chaperones. The daily small groups with adult leaders proved pivotal. Every year was the same. When we left the church on Monday morning, students were clustered with one another, as you would imagine. When we returned a week later, the student clusters were gone, and kids would argue about sitting with specific adults on the bus. It was magical to watch.

In the summer of 2003, an upcoming sophomore named Bradley reluctantly attended for the first time. Some friends convinced him to give it a try, and I think a pretty girl may also have influenced his decision. Bradley's life was changed. Even though his entire family attended our church, he had been emotionally distant from the church, faith, and relationships. That summer, in what he later called his Damascus Road encounter, he met the real Jesus face-to-face. He had connected deeply with Joe, his adult small group leader at the conference. Bradley identified with Joe's childhood, and after returning home, he wanted Joe to baptize him—an exciting first for Joe.

By the following Sunday, however, things had changed. Bradley told Joe his mom and dad had put the brakes on his baptism. Excitement turned to disappointment. Passion began to slip away. Bradley knew he could be baptized later in life, but a kid's energy can be zapped in an instant when adults don't see things the same way.

A few days later, Bradley's parents showed up in my office, heartbroken over his decision to be baptized by Joe. I was thoroughly confused.

"Nothing against Joe," Bradley's father explained. "I like him. He's been a friend for years. It's just that . . . we always thought we would be the ones to baptize our kids. We always read the Bible together as a family. We've made sure our kids know we are here for them, for anything they ask. I don't understand why he would ask Joe and not me. I mean, I'm supposed to be my kid's spiritual influence, right?"

I nodded with empathy. Then I caught them both off guard: "You two may be the greatest voice of influence in your children's lives, but you are not the only such voice."

"No," Bradley's mother replied, bewildered. "We're called to be the primary spiritual influence in our children's lives. We just did a Bible study series about that."

"Yes," I replied, "the primary, but not the only."

I explained The Shift to them and clarified that they needed to see the value of other caring adults speaking truth into their son's life.

And that's the key in this chapter. We are zeroing in on the post-Shift season when our influence ranking has dropped. We all feel the strong tendency to fight for control, command good behavior, or try to win our children by being their buddies. But these just open a canyon between us and our child. In fact, it sometimes causes irreparable damage. As I write, I'm in the middle of this season with my teenage daughters. Just this morning, as my fifteen-year-old rolled her eyes and argued with me, I had to remind myself that I am not the only voice of influence in her life.

If you have suddenly awakened to this harsh reality, what do you do? You widen the circle of influence in your child's life by amplifying other constructive voices. Celebrate those individuals. Encourage them. Champion them. Give thanks for every coach, small group leader, teacher, next-door neighbor, aunt or uncle, Sunday school teacher, troop leader, youth pastor, tutor, mentor, and friend who cares enough to invest in your child's life.

What Does a Wide Circle of Influence Look Like?

This may be a new concept for you, but consider all the caring people the Lord has placed in your child's life besides you. Don't dismiss their influence. They are not competitors to resist or compete with. You can't fix everything for your child; you need allies to help you. If you resist other good voices, you will neglect valuable voices and perspectives that your children need to hear.

It took me some time to acknowledge the importance of amplifying other voices of influence for my kids, intentionally inviting other caring adults to join me in speaking into my children's lives. But when I reached that stage, I discovered how much I needed others to reinforce my messages to my kids. Kristin and I discovered personally not that long ago just how crucial it is to form a wider circle of influence in our children's lives. One of our teenage daughters had been going through an extremely tough time, and it had left some serious tension between her and us. I am putting this lightly; it was actually excruciating. Even after all the previous years I had led teenagers through youth ministry, counseled hundreds of families in twenty years working in the church, and parented my two oldest daughters through their teen years more than a decade ago, I felt completely unprepared for this second round. It actually felt quite hopeless. I found myself often feeling overwhelmed. That was until our daughter went to spend a few days with our good friends, John and Nicole. John and Nicole are more like brother and sister to us than just close friends. We've known them the entire time we've lived in Indiana (which has been almost twenty years now). They are raising children the same ages we are. As they too are foster and adoptive parents, so we have very similar parenting journeys. Nicole was aware of the struggles we were having with our daughter. And at the right time, when she was at their house, Nicole spoke truth to her. The same truth, in fact, that we had been speaking to her for months. But this time, having another caring adult involved in her life, it resonated. She came home very apologetic and with a clear picture of what she had been doing. We weren't intimidated nor frustrated that she listened to another adult over us. We were grateful. This has been our dream for our kids for as long as they have been alive. We've yearned for other voices of influence to speak into their lives.

I'm not saying that we won't circle back around at some point and struggle with our child. We still have a long way to go. But Nicole, who is a part of our wide circle of influence, accomplished in one hour what had taken us months to try to communicate to our child. That is a parenting win as far as we're concerned.

We can't do this parenting gig alone, especially in competition with culture and our children's friends. (Neither of these is necessarily bad. Remember this when you want to condemn culture or your kids' friends because you don't understand them.) We can either fight to be heard or we can choose to partner with other voices. Which will you choose?

Joiner and Nieuwhof in *Parenting Beyond Your Capacity* point out a glaring truth that parents need to understand: "Regardless of your stage of parenting, we promise you one thing: a time will come when you and your children will need another adult in their lives besides you."[1]

I love that they use the word *need*. Because it is a need, not just a want. We won't see eye to eye with our child on everything. Our child may not feel comfortable talking to us about deep life questions. That's okay. By all means make the time to listen if they do open up. We still need to allow time to be present for our kids, to be willing to listen. But don't be offended if they turn to someone else. That's a win.

Joiner relates how his son chose to tell his small group leader something about a girl he liked that he didn't want to tell his father. It wasn't easy for Joiner. It may have grieved him deeply. But Joiner said his son "needed more than a parent. He needed somebody who cared about him but who was not responsible for him. He needed somebody who would say what I would say as his parent but who didn't make the rules."[2] When he realized this need in his son, he found peace in allowing another caring adult's investment in his child.

If more parents would come to this realization, I believe many parent-teen relationships would find themselves on a different trajectory. Bradley needed the same thing from his small group leader Joe that Joiner's son needed. I wish Bradley's parents had discovered that. Teenagers need advice, perspective, and guidance from other adults who believe and say the same things their parents do but who don't have the same authority as their parents.

Older kids need a *mentor*—not another buddy, but a guide. When life seems out of control and makes no sense—which is just about every day for many teens—our child may listen to someone who is not us. This is why the BFF parenting approach poses danger. Parents who think they are fully sufficient to meet this need will neglect the means God has provided to meet it—other lighthouses to show kids the way through the storm and away from the rocks.

Our children are exploring what it means to have their own faith, their own ideals, and their own beliefs. It's good when there are other adults to help them find their way. Recently, our seventeen-year-old daughter began dating. We were a little uneasy that the baby we adopted at three was suddenly hanging out alone with the opposite sex. But we were confident she was in good hands because she told us she was continually talking with her small group leader at church. We could sleep at ease, knowing that another voice of influence, who wasn't us but who upheld our values, was speaking into her life.

Once again, if you are beating yourself up because of failures in the past, don't. We've all failed. Parenting is an unending series of lessons. We all have to learn new concepts or principles. We all need to step into the light at one point or another, sometimes after years in the dark. That's not just parenting—that's life.

How to Widen the Circle

How can you best enlarge your children's circles of influence?

1. *Amplify healthy voices.* Choose or advocate for people of character who live with integrity and a solid moral compass, who have a compelling faith, who are loving and will listen without criticizing or judging, and who won't take sides or buy into family drama. They have the wisdom to point your child toward healthy ways of thinking and living. Exercise due diligence to ensure healthy voices of influence.

2. *Amplify the voices of those who reflect your heart.* They may not possess your authority, but choose individuals who reflect your values and desires for your child. As a youth pastor, I always got to know my students' parents, particularly the parents of boys in my small group. I wanted to know their hearts as well as my students' hearts. I never wanted to contradict a parent.

95

Do the other adults in your child's life reflect your heart for your child?

3. *Advocate for small groups for kids.* When I was a youth pastor, we put most of our resources into training and equipping small group leaders whose passion was to pour into and mentor junior high and high school students. If you are not in a church or faith-based community that invests in small group leaders, it's time to find a different church. I am being blunt about this because this is your child's heart we're talking about.

4. *Celebrate and reinforce the need for community among parents.* I am a big believer in connecting to a wide community of like-minded people. Kristin and I know, eight times over, that the adoption journey is unusual. Because of the trauma some of our kiddos have experienced in the past, we deal with issues most parents don't. Therefore, most people don't understand why we parent the way we do. We have found it essential to be part of a community of those who do understand. We depend on them and glean from them. You need to connect with people who understand your parenting scenario. If you are a Christian, connect with an authentic community of Christ followers.

Many factors play into amplifying voices of influence. And your circle may include adults outside of your place of worship—maybe a coach, teacher, or family member. Be sure to evaluate each one carefully.

Pause to Reflect

1. What are your initial thoughts about amplifying other voices of influence? Do you agree? Disagree? Struggle with the idea? Why is this?

2. How have you amplified other voices of influence and widened the circle of influence in your child's life? Or how will you plan to do this?

3. What are the biggest benefits to widening the circle?

4. Write down names of caring adults who could be part of this wider circle for your child.

8

Time Is Not on Your Side

Key 4: Use Your Time Wisely

A couple of years ago, I was invited by a friend to speak at a holiday dinner for coaches and administrators of a local high school in central Indiana. The only criterion was to "make it challenging and encouraging."

I can do that, I thought.

As the event drew closer, however, I found myself struggling with what I was going to say. I wrote, then erased, then wrote some more, then balled up the page and tossed it in the trash. I paced back and forth in my home office. I even reached out to my friend to ask a few more questions about the audience—coaches, teachers, and school administrators—and the intent of the gathering.

This went on for a couple of weeks until the dinner was just a few days away. I was nervous. I had previously spoken only to parents, so this would be a challenge. As I wrestled with what to say, I often looked at my iCalendar. Each time, I said, "I'm running out of time."

And finally it hit me—*time*!

There's so little of it, I thought. *It's fleeting. Before long these teachers, coaches, and administrators will watch the students in their care walk out their doors forever. That's what I need to talk about.* I decided to challenge them to use their remaining time wisely, to understand the power of their influence over their students, and to make the most of every day.

I used the metaphor of a football game—a good approach for coaches, who understand game time. A football game starts with four full quarters. Plenty of time, right? Most coaches don't start by focusing heavily on clock management (although the good ones still pay attention to the time). Even in the locker room at halftime, many think they have all the time in the world. They strategize, scheme, and motivate the team to play harder or differently.

But once the fourth quarter starts, they have to pay attention to the clock. It's time to utilize every minute of possession. It's time for their defense to force the opposing offense to go three and out in order for their offense to get the ball back. They need to be wise, making the most of the final opportunities they are given, because before they know it, the game will be over. The final seconds will run out, and the time leading up to that moment will be tucked into history forever, never to return, no second chances.

I challenged my audience to maximize their time with their students, many of whom were athletes. I urged them to take every opportunity to pour into the kids, instruct them, and lead them. Most importantly, I presented my case that they do all they can for maximum influence.

This is my challenge to you. As parents, you don't really have much time with your child. But you look at your newborn son or daughter and think time is not an issue, at least not right now. Few of us truly consider how fast time goes.

As our parents said to Kristin and me, your parents or another seasoned parent may have said to you, "Time goes by fast. Before you know it, she's all grown up and you are moving her into college," but you dismissed or downplayed it. We did.

Parents fit into one of two categories. Either they anticipate high school graduation eighteen years away and want to spend all the time they can with their child, or they think that it's all so far away they don't need to worry about missing opportunities with their child.

When our firstborn daughter lay sleeping in her bassinet in 2002, we didn't think about the limited time we had with her in our home. When we set up a college fund in 2003, even our investment guy warned us.

I thought, *I've got years!*

In middle school? Didn't even give it a thought. High school? Not on our radar. And college still seemed light-years away.

Then I blinked, and she was two years from college.

It's natural for parents not to think that far ahead. We did the same with our daughter who came to live with us at age three. But thanks to Facebook Memories, a picture popped up just the other day—our two girls in princess dresses, headed out to the daddy-daughter dance eight years ago. In my mind, that was last year.

Yep, that fast. Now two of them are high school juniors. I'm in the fourth quarter, the eleventh hour, so I'm finally paying attention to the clock. I'm making sure every moment counts. I can't go back in time and leave work early to attend a tea party in my daughter's bedroom, surrounded by her stuffed animals and Barbies. I can't rewind the clock, grab my baseball glove, and toss the ball with my son in the side yard until sunset.

Thankfully, I actually did all those things at those times, so I don't carry around much regret. But thinking back on those moments brings into perspective just how fast time is moving.

If time is flying, and we have a limited supply of it with our children, what should we do? I'm going to suggest a perspective shift for you, beginning the moment your children are born or adopted. It's critical that you keep this perspective as your children grow and become preteens, junior highers, and high schoolers. Understanding this shift in perspective is as important as understanding The Shift of influence I described earlier. It's a game changer for connecting with your child.

The Quantity of Quality Times

One of my sons loves—I mean *loves*—to go to the grocery store with us. When he gets wind of an upcoming trip to the grocery store, even just to get milk or gas, he comes bounding out the front door to join us. He's helpful and a joy to have along.

It took me awhile to realize how much he loved going with us. I wasn't opposed to my son coming; I just didn't consider the significance of these small moments with him. When I worked full-time in a church, I was gone from home eight to ten hours a day. I missed a great deal with my kids—walks in the park, soccer practice, cooking dinner together, playing in the backyard, listening to how their day at school went. And when I finally arrived home after a sometimes mentally and emotionally exhausting day, I was more like a zombie than an engaged father. I hated being in that condition. Still do. During my last season of working outside the home—nearly five years ago now—I was busier and more consumed than in the previous thirteen years of ministry. I was working in a church that was spiraling downward. There were many difficulties among the leadership and in the congregation. Staff were being fired to make up for financial loss, and people were angrily beating down our doors, figuratively and literally, for answers as to why a beloved staff member was suddenly gone. The leadership made relatively good decisions behind closed doors but then communicated them poorly. Entire sections of the building were closed to save on utilities, and I was physically and mentally exhausted by endless meetings. I couldn't take any more.

In January, I began looking often at my calendar and fantasizing about my week of vacation in April—loading up our twelve-passenger van, driving south to Florida, and leaving all this behind. We might even stay two weeks if we were having too much fun to return to real life. On those winter nights when I was slammed at the office, I would glance at that calendar and think, *I'm going to sacrifice time at home now, stay buckled down, and when I get to Florida in April, I'll spend quality time with my family. Just three months to go and the payoff will be great.* So that's what I did. I worked and worked and worked.

But my plan had a problem. I was immersed in work for so long, sacrificing time with my family, that it was difficult for me to shut it off during vacation. In fact, when we were about to head south, Kristin and one of our daughters had to tell me *to turn off my phone*. Ouch! And when we arrived at our vacation house, I felt as though I didn't know these people, even though we lived under the same roof.

You see, I had spent months plowing ahead with work—hours and days and weeks on end—with the goal of spending quality time in Florida, but I had missed all the days between with my children. I had sacrificed the smaller, seemingly unimportant moments with my children along the way. Sitting next to my daughter as she worked through math problems. A movie night after homework and baths. A trip to the post office to drop off mail.

I misunderstood what quality time really was. A big vacation is great, but I failed to realize the significance of the smaller everyday moments. They are quality time, and they add up.

Joiner and Nieuwhof point out, "It's not the quantity or quality times you need as a family—it's the quantity of quality times."[1] How much time with our kids will we sacrifice between vacations? And will we still know our kids when we get to that vacation?

Remember the importance of the quantity of quality times—the many small moments to be with your kids, listen to their hearts, and know them as fellow human beings. At the end of my life, I want to look back and be able to say that I knew my kids because I paid attention during the in-between times.

You may be wondering, *What about my teenager who doesn't seem to want to do anything with me, let alone listen to a word I say or have a conversation with me?* I hear that question every time I speak or write on maximizing time with your child. It's a big struggle that many parents face. But the answer is simple: tie them up with duct tape, place them in your car, force them to ride along with you, and tell them, "You will spend time with me or you won't come home!"

I'm just kidding, of course. We both know that won't work (and it's illegal in most states).

Here is the real answer: you must readjust your expectations and relationship with your teenager, at least for a season.

Maximizing Time with Your Teenager

Kristin and I get it. We understand how difficult this season can be because we are in the trenches with you. We too are trying to figure out the moods, eye rolls, and extreme emotions of our kids as well as attempting normal relationships with them.

My fifteen-year-old daughter used to be excited to ride with us anywhere we were headed, and when she was four we thought that would never end. Now she's a teenager with her own thoughts on politics, beliefs, fashion trends, what Taylor Swift posted on Instagram, her math teacher's ridiculous one-liners, and whether she wants to get married someday. Bottom line: she's becoming a young adult. She no longer plays with Barbies, hosts tea parties with stuffed animals as guests, or parades through the living room in Disney Princess dresses. My daddy heart longs for those days, but they are locked in the past, living only in my memory. She's a freethinking, smart, levelheaded teenager. She doesn't need me or her mom as much as she used to. This is all predictable and natural.

So how do you make the most of your time with your teenage child?

1. *Adjust your expectations.* The fact is your kid is not a child anymore. You can't expect your fifteen- or sixteen-year-old to relate to you the way they did in elementary school. Interactions naturally become different. Coming with us to run a spontaneous errand isn't an option now. We still expect full participation in certain family events. Holidays and birthday parties are required attendance. But we understand our daughter would rather watch *Pretty Little Liars* than join us on an errand in which she has no interest. Adjust your expectations.

2. *Keep their responses in perspective.* When your kid declines to do something with you, it's easy to feel rejected, especially with children who clung to you before. After years with little separation, The Shift is difficult, and new responses are easy to take personally. I finally realized my daughter wasn't saying no to me. She was saying no to something she wasn't interested in. It's that simple. Likewise, my son isn't turning down time with me; he just doesn't appreciate a store that doesn't sell Hot Wheels cars. We love our kids, and our soft hearts can take personally a response that isn't personal after all. Consider age appropriateness and your kids' changing interests and priorities.

3. *Relate to them on their level.* This does *not* mean you resort to being Buddy the elf. It means you willingly step into their world and listen to their hearts, even if you don't completely understand their reasoning or pop

culture lingo. My daughter, like millions of others, follows an internet sensation and vlogger named Jake Paul on YouTube and Instagram. She's basically a walking library on everything Jake Paul. I, however, am not. But I know more about him now because when I'm driving my daughter to school she tells me all about the stunts he pulls. She plays audio for me during our ten-minute commute. I listen and laugh with her. Sometimes I'll ask questions. Sometimes I just listen and react to her reactions. I will never be a Jake Paul fan. But I'm a fan of my daughter, and I follow who she is. I love learning all about her heart and mind, so I'm tuned in when she talks about Jake Paul, or anything else. I am privileged to be an invited guest into her world. I take every opportunity I'm given to relate at her level. Take these opportunities when and where you can get them.

4. *Seize the small moments.* We have so many small moments with our children. If only we would open our eyes more often and recognize what is right before us. I'm speaking to me and you. Maybe you've conceded that your teenagers want nothing more than to avoid individual time with you. But maybe they want that time more than you realize. Don't fast-track your assumptions without knowing for sure. Yes, create and maximize those big, elaborate together times, but the small moments add up to big impact too. Chances are your adult child will recount the small moments as often as the big ones. Just the other night our teenager unexpectedly asked us to tuck her into bed. You better believe we seized the moment.

5. *Maintain control of your emotions.* When your kid seems to operate on a different wavelength, don't over-react or become forceful. Even the not-so-rosy times are opportunities to love and celebrate your child for who they are and who they are becoming. Respond with kindness, peacefully and full of grace. Pay attention to your tone and your word choices, saving up change in the relational bank, which you will need later.

You'll Never Know If You Never Ask

I mentioned fast-tracking your assumptions. When my teen-ager isn't rising up and calling me blessed, when her face isn't glowing with an adoring "Yes, Daddy" look, I am quick to throw my hands up and conclude that she has lost all interest in me. But there are many other ways to interpret the behavior of this complex young person—a thinking, feeling, believing, self-determining human being. Unfortunately, many of us believe our kids hate us just because they are moody. Perhaps instead they are caught in the vortex of humanness—between childhood and adulthood—trying to figure out how to navigate life. But in my insecurity I make it all about me. I have to remember that once upon a time I too was a moody, snot-nosed kid who made my parents think I hated them. So were you. Our child may simply have had a bad day. But if we keep jumping to the conclusion that the relationship will never get any better, guess what? It won't.

Remember that your kids are trying to figure out who they are in a confusing, messed-up world. Keep on pursuing them through their moods, in spite of what you are tempted to think. You may just achieve a different outcome. Ask them to spend time with you in all kinds of old and new ways. And when they do, surprise them with a stop at Starbucks or for ice cream. They may say no thanks to your invite, but you'll never know (or go) if you never ask.

A few weeks ago I was gearing up for a ten-day trip, preparing for multiple speaking engagements. The content preparation and planning kept me buried, getting up before sunup and returning home after the kids' bedtime. I saw my kids in the course of this time period, but sparsely. One afternoon I planned on running to FedEx to print hundreds of booklets and name badges when one of my teenage daughters returned home from school. We talked a little, and I spontaneously asked if she wanted to tag along. I fully expected her to say no after her long school day, but to my surprise she said yes. I was caught off guard for a moment, but then I grabbed what I needed and we left.

My daughter had no interest in going into FedEx with me and stayed in the car, listening to music and texting friends. But as we drove there and back, we talked—a lot. Nothing earth shattering was said, but it was an hour that was beyond meaningful.

Quantity of quality time. Prioritizing family first, especially in the small moments. This makes all the difference in your relationships with your children. This can win their hearts.

Disrupters of Time

Even as I type these words, an enemy lurks, an enemy that feeds on our time. It lies in wait to pounce, eager to disrupt me and divert my attention from what matters most. Its common name is *distraction*, and it runs rampant in our culture through the internet and smartphone technology. It yearns to take me to the dark side, where I squander attention and affection on social media, text messages, emails, the *USA Today* app, YouTube clips, and the Weather Channel. This enemy stalks you too, circling constantly, waiting to strike. It may manifest as an iPhone, laptop, iPad, or TV. Or maybe *Sports Illustrated* or the newspaper. It wants to disrupt everything good about your home, especially your attention to your children. We may think we're being sly when we give in, but our kids aren't fooled. They know when we're not paying attention, or worse, paying half attention.

We live in the most distracted generation in all of human history. Never before has anyone had access to so much technology, up-to-date information, and high content-download speed. We can no longer claim ignorance because information screams at us from multiple devices in our homes and everywhere else. According to Statista, by 2021 social media networking and usage is expected to reach a staggering 3.02 billion users.[2] From January 2013 to September 2017, the number of monthly Instagram users rose from ninety million to eight hundred million.[3] That's fewer than five years! As of July 2018, Facebook has almost 2.2 billion monthly users and YouTube has 1.9 billion.[4] That's a huge number of people using a variety of social media every month.

Social media is useful, but it can be a big distraction, bleeding away our parenting time and effectiveness. A 2012 *Wall Street Journal* video report revealed a correlation during the years 2007–10 between increased smartphone use and increases in injuries to children on playground and nursery equipment.[5] In other words, caregivers using phones for various purposes are distracted while caring for children. I have to wonder about the correlation between children's emotional states and parents' use of devices and social media at home or anywhere else they should be attending to their kids. How have we hurt our children's hearts through these distractions? I'm guilty as charged. My family has called me on it, but they've forgiven me too.

I believe that email, texting, social media, and the internet are useful and important. So how do we utilize something that is important to our lives while ensuring that our families know beyond a shadow of a doubt they are our top priority? Three things come to mind.

Boundaries

We need to say no more often than we say yes to the use of social media. Our time is precious and fleeting, and we need to set strong boundaries around our work, hobbies, and other interests in order to give adequate time and full attention to our families. Boundaries are crucial to many aspects of healthy living, and chaos results from their absence. Let me state it bluntly: *When you are with your kids, put down your phone and log off email, social media, and web browsing.* It's that simple. And yes, I know it's hard.

Schedule your day intentionally. Set aside a specific time to go online to check Facebook, Instagram, and Twitter and to watch YouTube. Today, many of us may even need some of these media platforms to do our jobs. But we need to set limitations. So be intentional. Then come to a hard stop and have undistracted family time so that your children will know you are dialed in to them.

Priorities

Priorities reflect what is most important to us, what holds greatest value in our lives and hearts. Jesus said, "Wherever your treasure is, there the desires of your heart will also be" (Matt. 6:21). That's an age-old truth many of us remember from preschool Sunday school class, and it comes to life in fullest fashion—through our priorities and what we value most—when we become parents.

One way I show my family they are my priority is when I show up on time for various events. Being late, especially if it happens often, tells my wife and kids that something else is a higher priority to me than they are.

We all need to take a hard look at our priorities and re-order them where needed. We need to stop giving ourselves permission to place other things higher than our family. This can be hard, but it's crucial to winning our family's hearts. We must consciously and intentionally choose to make our kids a top priority in our lives. I'm historically bad at prioritizing my time, and that infiltrates my home life. I squander time on unimportant things and often leave little to no time to focus on my kids. Kristin is good at challenging me. Sometimes I need time to digest her confrontations, but they are always good for me and always help me grow.

Listening

Listening may sound elementary and obvious, but our generation has become awful at actively listening. Trust me, I'm talking to myself here as well as you. I sometimes think I'm listening when I'm really not. I've mastered the art of nodding while keeping an eye on the television or phone. I capture key words from a speaker and then attempt to form a commentary on them. But I'm not fooling anyone. I'm learning every day how to listen better, especially by putting down my phone. Just this morning one of my daughters wanted to tell me about the movie she was going to see with her friends. Fortunately, my phone was in a different room. I looked her in the eye, acknowledged she was talking to me, and engaged her with genuine questions and commentary. After she left for school, I reflected on that moment. It lasted all of five minutes, but it felt good to connect and actively listen to her heart and thoughts. The more I engage like this, the more likely she will want to share. That's a win!

Pause to Reflect

1. To what do you give most of your time? Be honest.

2. How have you seized the small quantities of time with your children that end up becoming quality? In what new ways might you do this?

3. What have been the biggest disrupters of your time with your children? How can you conquer them?

4. How can you incorporate boundaries and set priorities in your schedule to protect time to fully focus on your family?

9

Be Fully There

Key 5: Stay Involved with Your Kids

It was one of those warm Indiana days you cherish because you know summer has finally arrived. Even fifteen years later, I remember the baccalaureate service well because the master of ceremonies introduced the keynote speaker and his wife as "dedicated and involved parents, taking an active role in their children's lives."

Dedicated and involved. Those words rang in the ears of this young father. *I want to be that kind of parent,* I thought. *I want someone to say that about me.* At the time, Kristin and I had only one child, a one-year-old, and in that moment my mind focused on my baby girl. How desperately I wanted her to know how much I loved her and how committed I was to being involved in her life.

Dedicated and involved. Those words have motivated me for nearly fifteen years now. They've become a silent mantra

I keep tucked away in the depths of my heart and mind as I work hard to relate to my children, to know them, and to be interested in them as they grow into adults. I don't want to look back and say that I missed a moment because I was consumed with work or distracted by something superficial on Facebook or Instagram.

Involvement is a critical piece of parenting. I could write an entire book on this subject alone because I believe it's an umbrella over every other aspect of influential parenting.

Why Involvement Wins the Heart

First and foremost, active involvement is a gateway to personal, relational knowledge—it gives you the opportunity to know your child. You can't know someone you are not involved with. Being fully present in your child's life allows you to know intimate details about them—their likes, dislikes, dreams, fears, struggles, and interests. You learn about their personal beliefs, friendships, passions, favorite television show, college choices, career aspirations, favorite musician or YouTuber and why he's "soooo cute," what's happening on social media, which teachers irritate them and why, and what they think about God. You'll discover what they think about social issues such as gender equality and same-sex marriage, what book they are reading, which iPhone app they are currently into, and more.

You may squirm as you read this list, but it's a snapshot of their world. These things are what make your teenagers tick. Like it or not, they live in an active and real culture that is coming at them one thousand miles an hour through mass media, technology that changes almost daily, and immense

116

pressure to measure up in a society that keeps changing the rules. You can resist and deny it. Or you can press into it and learn about their culture—and thereby learn about them! This will give you an all-access pass to become influential in their lives. Time is precious and moves quickly.

Second, active involvement allows you to sow valuable seeds of relationship. The more opportunities you take, the deeper the relational roots will grow into their hearts. Picture your relationships with your kids like a farmer who watches and carefully tends his crops, patiently trusting that the slow growth process is going on above and below the surface, even when the change is imperceptible. Someday, you will relate to your son or daughter as a fellow adult. That future relationship can be rich and alive if you commit now to being actively involved in your child's life.

What Does Active Involvement Look Like?

What does it mean, day in and day out, to play an active role with your children? Here are some practical ideas.

Carve Out Time to Listen

Listening is the biggest indicator of active involvement. The way you get to know a close friend is to listen. The way you learn how to do something new is to listen to instructions. The way you get to know your children is to listen to them. And this requires that you intentionally carve out time to do so. There are many ways to create time to listen. For example, in my family we make sure we eat together around our table several times each week, no cell phones or any other distractions allowed that might hinder open conversation. We allow each person an opportunity to share. At bedtime, we sit on the edge of each kid's bed to listen to a story from his or her day. There is no magic formula. Look at your day and plan this out. And be ready to set aside what you are doing when your children want to talk.

Set Aside Distracting Devices

Turn off or silence your phone, shut down your Facebook page, and leave the car radio off when you are devoting your attention to your child. You can't converse with them when you are talking to someone else or catching up on Instagram. Those things can wait until later. Right now your children are there, needing your full attention, and your time with them is fleeting. Don't let meaningless stuff fill your time. Let *your children* fill your time.

Date Your Child

That's right, date your kid! Intentionally schedule time to go out with your son or daughter. Take them to get coffee, for a special mom-and-me or dad-and-me dinner, or to shop. I've mentioned the importance of making the most of small moments, such as running errands together. But dating your children is different; you are more intentionally focused on them with the purpose of giving them your full attention and learning about them. Even if you think your child won't want to do this, try it. You may be surprised, especially if they don't see it coming. One of my favorite Instagram posts is from author and blogger Jen Hatmaker. It's a photo of her college-age son with the caption: "Having coffee with this son baby at my favorite place and I love everything and everyone. I have him for six days. I will feed him whatever he wants and slip him cash and trash talk the professors he hates. He can do no wrong this week and no one can tell me otherwise."[1] I immediately thought, *That's how you involve yourself in your child's life.*

Make Even Small Investments

Do the large and small favors and courtesies for your children that show them they are important to you. When we decided to forsake the confines of suburbia and move to rural Indiana—where we could light things on fire, make as much noise as we wanted, and allow our young sons to roam the backyard in their underwear—we chose to buy property near our previous hometown where our daughters' friends lived. We promised our daughters, "We will drive you to your friends' homes, and if your friends need rides, we will be glad to pick them up." We took for granted that other parents would do the same. We were wrong. We have been shocked that other parents avoid becoming involved with their children in these simple ways. Many parents refuse to pick up their children from our home just a mile or two away. Or they go to bed before their kids are safely home. I'm not being judgmental, but I don't get it. I believe doing these kinds of things as part of our involvement in our children's lives are small investments that can have big significance.

Encourage Transparency with Minimal Correction

There is a time for correcting your children's bad choices. Kids need boundaries and consequences, as we've already discussed. But for the sake of relationship, sometimes you need to actively listen and participate without immediately jumping to correction. Let them share what ticks them off, which teacher they can't stand, which popular boy at school is actually a total jerk, who got busted for their social media post, or what they think about politics. Kids, especially teenagers, need to feel safe with their parents. Your necessary role as disciplinarians doesn't mean you can't allow them an outlet. Kristin and I give our teenagers permission to share frustrations and fears, and I cherish the moments when they do. Sometimes we need to remind them to watch their language or to be nicer, but we never stifle transparency, and this creates an environment in which they feel safe to share openly. My mom wasn't a perfect parent, but this was one thing she did right. My sister and I could always share our feelings without fear of judgment. That forged in us confidence and honesty that continue today. I even founded a blog called *Confessions of an Adoptive Parent*.

What about My "Littles"?

If your children are young, and you are still early in the parenting journey but you are starting to think in advance about the road ahead, good for you! Many parents don't do this, and they are usually the ones who end up in my office for help. This chapter fits your season of parenting because involvement must begin in the early childhood years. Even your very young children are listening and watching and can understand what's going on. They are listening, and they want *you* to listen to *them*!

Highlight those last seven words: *they want you to listen to them.* Write them down and put them where you'll see them every day. To be involved with your kids, you must *listen to your children at every age.*

Don't neglect the importance of conversations with your littles (as one of our team members refers to her young children). Conversation is healthy, even if it surrounds Sponge-Bob or Dora the Explorer. Learn their perspective. Put down the cell phone or turn off the car radio—they know when you are distracted. And by all means, show up for their activities. I'm grateful that, when our firstborn daughter was just a baby, Kristin and I made a commitment to be involved in her life. That led to many conversations about Barbie and *The Suite Life of Zack and Cody*, giving her permission to talk honestly with her mom and dad. That has paved the way for openness with us now during her teens.

Note that we didn't just *appear* to be interested; we *were* interested. We didn't fake our involvement; we *were* involved. Often, we adults become good actors with our littles, responding with "Uh-huh" or "Wow, really, that's amazing!" when our children are trying to tell us something that is important to them. If this is you, don't beat yourself up. In this world we tend to be consumed with our own interests and give our children canned answers. But we need to make a point to stop doing this. When we pay close attention beginning in the early days, the soil of our relationship grows richer with each passing year.

Pause to Reflect

1. Evaluate your schedule, your priorities, and your focus. Be honest with yourself. How much time do you spend actively involved with your children?

2. What do you need to eliminate or reprioritize in order to be more involved in your children's activities, hobbies, or interests?

3. Why is involvement crucial to your children's health and positive growth?

4. Write down a few (realistic) promises you are willing to make to yourself and your children in order to become more involved in their lives.

10

I Would Rather Be the Tortoise

Key 6: Commit to Consistency

If you haven't heard the story "The Tortoise and the Hare," welcome to planet Earth. (Kidding!) Just in case, here's my short version. The hare (read "rabbit") ridicules the tortoise (fancy for "turtle") for being so slow. The tortoise decides he's had enough, and he challenges the hare to a race. The outcome is obvious. Give the tortoise a million chances, and a million times the hare wins. The starting gun fires. The hare darts off, then stops for a nap, confident he'll wake in plenty of time to win. (Spoiler alert!) But the impossible happens. The hare wakes just in time to see his creeping contender win.

How in the world could this have happened? One word: *consistency*.

You see, the hare ran fast, then stopped, expecting his inconsistency to be inconsequential. But the tortoise never stopped, never varied his pace, never gave in to distraction or wandered off the path. Unceasing consistency was his secret weapon. It's not rocket science, yet many people miss it.

I try to exercise at a gym five days a week—around 5:00 a.m.—before my kids are up for school. You are probably thinking I'm crazy, but I love it. It's my favorite time of the day. My mind is clear, the day is dark and new, and the roads are empty. I get uninterrupted time to think, pray, listen, and just be. I wear noise-canceling headphones—God's gift to introverts—and spend my time drowning out the world.

I wasn't always this consistent. For the majority of my life, I've struggled with laziness, apathy, and self-discipline. Only in the last eight years have I gotten back in shape and stayed the course. Now I'm committed to heart health and longevity, caring for this one-time gift—my body. And consistency is the key.

Then January comes around. For two weeks, I stand in lines waiting for my favorite machines, usually behind someone with no clue how to work them, who will probably give up soon and never return. Here's my point: these people have one big problem, and it's not that they are overweight, out of shape, or unwilling. They lack consistency.

A few years ago I was talking with Harold, a man in his fifties or sixties. One New Year's Day, he decided to change his commitment to health, and he joined my gym. On a winter morning, I stepped onto a mountain-climbing machine next to him and began my usual thirty-five-minute workout. I set the resistance and incline fairly high, and as I began I heard a gasp. Harold was staring at my machine's display.

"How do you add that much resistance?" he asked. "I can't come anywhere close to that."

"Well," I replied, "I've been using this machine for the past five years. It was really hard in the beginning."

He paused thoughtfully. "How did you get to where you are now?"

"I just kept doing it over and over and adding resistance little by little."

"So consistency was your secret sauce?"

I nodded. "I guess that's it."

Can you guess one of the best examples of consistency I saw after that day? Harold. Morning after morning, Monday through Friday, Harold showed up and gutted it out until he surpassed many of the early morning exercisers. When the rest of us had finished and sat down, trying to catch our breath, Harold was still going strong. He had no previous history of great conditioning. He just made a new commitment and stuck with it.

Consistency is a game changer with the power to produce results like nothing else. Pay credit card bills consistently, and you will eventually pay them off. Water your lawn without fail, and it will turn green. Keep working at building a company or brand, and it will come to fruition. Same with writing a book.

This is never truer than in parenting. If we consistently love our kids, they will feel loved and be more secure human beings. If we are consistent with boundaries and appropriate discipline, kids will (usually) gain an understanding of right and wrong and the importance of setting their own boundaries. Consistently spending time with our kids will make them feel valued and will build solid relationships.

The Consistency Quiz

As a parent, ask yourself the following critical questions:

1. *Do I consistently show love to my children?* Of course you love your children, and that won't change. But do you *show* it so they know it? What shows love? Time is one of the biggest ways. We've covered this, but now put those precious large and small moments in the context of consistency. Keep on seizing them with no big gaps between. Here is another way to show love. One of my daughters had to tell us she was pregnant with no place to live, no job, and from a relationship with a guy she had not known long. We could have cast her out and told her to clean up her mess, but we didn't do that. We've been loved while in the middle of our messes, and this mercy often pays huge dividends—eventually. Sometimes, consistent love means you love and love and love and experience the rewards much later.

2. *Do I consistently take up a position of observer before instructor?* Are you so busy trying to teach your children that you've missed their hearts? Have you concerned yourself so much with being right that you've lost sight of the beautiful human beings your children are and are becoming? Often we choose to die on parenting hills that aren't worth the sacrifice. Recently, my sixteen-year-old wanted a piece of construction paper for listing her goals. I argued that she should use an index card instead, both to save paper and for the lines. We went back and forth until it dawned on me: *she wanted to do a responsible, grown-up thing—write a*

task list. I was missing her maturity because of a scrap of paper. I'm learning to observe, not just teach.

3. *Do I present consistent boundaries to my children?* I have learned this the hard way. Our kids are smart people, even at age four or five, and they can spot inconsistency right away. It's unfair—to them and me— when I outline a boundary but then get soft and don't enforce it consistently. Boundaries that work are solid, unless they were faulty in the first place. If curfew is ten o'clock, it's ten o'clock. No need for lecture or discussion. Say it and leave it. Your kid is smart enough to understand your words. And keep in mind that consistent, enforced boundaries help your children feel secure and loved. When they test those boundaries, whether they realize it or not, they are truly hoping you'll push back because they need the stability of your consistency. Every time you calmly stand your ground and say no, you add another drop of love to the ocean of their heart.

4. *Do I apply consistent consequences?* Sometimes love has to be tough, unfailing in truth, steadfast about what's right. Tough love can drain the life out of us when, in our children's best interests, we have to do something that feels uncompassionate but is something they truly need. When your child crosses a boundary you've established, pay attention to your reaction. Rather than lecture and shame, let a cold, hard consequence provide the teaching your child needs. But consequences need to be consistent. Stick to your guns: keep your child's cell phone the full two weeks; restrict driving the full

month and let your child walk. They will live! And they will definitely learn and grow. A lax consequence teaches your child not to take you seriously.

Wake Up, O Sleeper

Remember the hare? He started great, leaving a cloud of dust behind, while the tortoise stood there scratching his shell. The hare fully expected to beat the tortoise hands down. He was so confident he took a nap.

And lost.

Why did the inexplicable happen? Because of sleep.

Let me explain. Instead of persistently and consistently running the race before him, staying on task, engaging in his primary responsibility, the hare took a nap.

Now don't get me wrong; naps are not bad. I love naps. Kristin and I believe naps have been sent to earth directly by the hand of God for parents. (Along with wine, but that's another story.) But for the hare, a nap was irresponsible and detrimental to success. He lost as a result of his careless lapse.

How often has "sleep" distracted us from our focus on the most important things in life? I'm not talking about literal sleep but rather figurative slumber—lapsing in consistency, relaxing our vigilance, closing our eyes to reality, and being inattentive when we need most to engage our kids. Absence when our presence is needed. Lack of focus when we need eyes fixed on the path. Stalling out when we should keep moving toward our family's future.

These lapses can occur easily and for many reasons in today's world. Most importantly, The Shift in influence can catch us asleep if we misunderstand it or fail to embrace it. When it seems our children care about everything and everyone else but us, we may passively give up rather than actively engage them when it's most needed. In confusion, we stop communicating and concede defeat. It's like a scene from the 2005 film *Mr. and Mrs. Smith* starring Angelina Jolie and Brad Pitt. Mrs. Smith says to a therapist, "I feel like the space between us has filled up with everything we don't say to each other."[1] How often does this happen with us and our teenage kids? Often!

Usually, we don't even realize we've fallen asleep until we wake up to our family's peril. Our kids are lost, and the life we thought we were living has suddenly crumbled around us. We look around, bewildered by what we see. Think about how often spouses suddenly leave, walk out on their marriages, seemingly without warning. The remaining spouse is left standing alone in an empty house, crushed and wondering how this could have happened. But the warnings were there. It's just that the spouse left behind was asleep, unaware, maybe too focused on everything happening around them to see what was happening right before them. As parents, we need to consistently engage our kids more than ever during their preteen, junior high, and high school years. That's when they need us most, even if it doesn't appear so. Remember, even in the fourth place of influence you are still on the list, and you have a responsibility to be active and consistent in their lives.

Never has this been truer than in my own family. In early 2014, we realized we had been sleeping. The walls of our home, which we thought were secure and intact, were collapsing. It began when one of my children confessed to my wife that in the middle of the night she often thought about ways to kill herself. This opened our eyes to an entirely new reality. Our girl was suffering from a dark, quiet depression because of our volatile home environment. Its main contributor was my oldest son, who suffers from alcohol-related neurodevelopmental disorder (ARND), which is on the spectrum of fetal alcohol syndrome. His birth mother had consumed drugs and alcohol during her pregnancy, leaving his brain permanently damaged. We adopted him at thirteen months. His prefrontal cortex, which is responsible for logic, reasoning, self-control, and impulse control, was not functioning properly, resulting in violent outbursts, destruction of property, and often bodily harm, mainly to Kristin and me. We had to be vigilant 24–7, 365 days a year. This environment triggered our daughter's depression.

We soon found ourselves the subject of a Child Protective Services investigation due to one of our other kids' poor choices. This season has gone down in our family's history as the darkest we have faced. We lived in anxiety, always worried that someone would show up and take all our kids away. It was one of the worst feelings in the world. At the same time, I took a cut in responsibility and salary at my church job, and we instantly found ourselves in a house we couldn't afford with bills stacking up by the week.

Our family was in shambles; we had lost our way. Kristin and I discovered we had been sleeping through life and parenting. Our kids were turning to unhealthy outlets for their stress. Our unquestioned norm was becoming consumption of stuff over true relationship. Something had to drastically change. We had to wake up. More than ever we needed to engage with our kids, and that's exactly what we decided to do.

We sold our way-too-expensive house and downsized from 4,300 square feet to a 1,950-square-foot farmhouse on the opposite side of town. We had way too many possessions in our house, so we sold or gave away many of them. We sold a car and got rid of most of our Christmas decorations, extra furniture, clothes—anything that wouldn't fit in our smaller home and shed. Good thing too because I would be fired in a few months' time—not because of anything I did. It was an extremely unhealthy place with poor leadership. (That transition pushed me to become a full-time blogger, author, and public speaker. I love my job!)

I would like to forget 2014 ever happened. But it was a year of awakening—a massive family turning point—and I'm grateful.

A Word about Waking Up

Waking up from slumbering in your parenting doesn't mean you go into Commander mode. This is a common knee-jerk reaction. You want to confiscate cell phones, cancel cable, fling the shades down, drive over CD collections, block every number in your kid's phone, and hunker down around a single candle in a dark basement singing hymns. (No? Okay, but you get the idea.)

When we woke up, we didn't become religious fanatics or oppressive rule enforcers as some might recommend. It's one thing to reinforce boundaries and outline the rules; it's another to go overboard with them. That's not an authentic or constructive way to approach family brokenness. And it's the opposite of how Jesus interacted with people. He never responded to a broken person with religious rhetoric or a rule-based plan of conduct. The Jesus we follow is wild and free and extravagantly loving. He deeply delights in us and our precious children, even though we have screwed up royally. That's exactly how we decided to respond to our kids. Even though they had made some serious mistakes, we did not let those define them. We looked at it this way: our biggest mistakes have never defined us, so our children's do not define them. There was no shame, no scorn, no contempt, and absolutely no lecturing. What good would it have done to allow the ugly stepsisters of parenting and all their friends to take up residence in our home? It would have done nothing to help our children through their darkness and wrestling and would have driven a wedge between us.

When you wake up, remember that your kids are human beings like you—flesh-and-blood, mistake-making human beings. So give your kids and yourselves a break. Remember to exercise your influence in loving, purposeful, constructive, affirming ways. Focus on your kids' hearts first, then on their behavior or choices. Remember that your goal is not to make your children march in line but to help them understand how to live in freedom. This happens through love, not just rules or restrictions.

Pause to Reflect

1. How could you become more consistent as a parent?

2. In particular, how will you more consistently seize large and small moments with your kids?

3. How will you more consistently set and enforce boundaries and consequences? How will you ensure that love is your motive in doing so?

4. In what ways have you remained awake and vigilant in your parenting? How have you been asleep?

11

Hollywood Lied!

Key 7: Love No Matter What

Love is an important part of influence and crucial for building a relationship with our child that lasts a lifetime. We use the word *love* many different ways. It's so watered down and overused in our society that it has become white noise. Love is the theme of just about every pop song and the driving plotline of many movies and television shows. We use *love* to describe our favorite outfit, our choice Starbucks drink, our iPhone, a boyfriend, a pet, a new car, or a job (sometimes).

I've rarely met a parent who wouldn't say they love their kiddos more than anything on earth. Whether we have created them biologically or they have come to us through adoption or fostering, we love them. Anything less would be inhuman. But while we may think our love is obvious, is it obvious to our children?

The old adage is true: *Actions speak louder than words.* The way we care for our children, the amount of time we spend with them, the interest we show in their lives, whether our computer or cell phone is more important to us (and trust me, they know)—these all reinforce their awareness of whether we love them.

But words are important too. Do we affirm and encourage our children? Do we tell them we believe in their strengths, their ability to make good choices, their potential? Do we celebrate their successes, their brilliance? How we say our words matters as well. What do we communicate through our tone?

Actions and words are married to one another. They are attached at the syllable. They dance together in the middle of our relationships, particularly with our children. Both are needed to make our love known to our children. Love is evident in the way we speak when our children have made big mistakes. Love shines through when we celebrate major victories with them or grieve devastating losses alongside them. Love leads the way when we must exercise tough love or reinforce a boundary that may not feel all warm and fuzzy. Love is the guiding light when we hold our broken, hurting children in our arms and tell them it's going to be all right and that Mommy and Daddy are not going anywhere.

Loving words and actions must hold hands tightly. You can't have one without the other. But our world doesn't tell us this about love. Movies, TV shows, and songs usually center on feelings—infatuation, surface emotions—or what someone is or isn't getting. Parent-child relationships are often portrayed in feel-good stories. Rarely do we see love that is raw and messy and that makes a sacrificial commitment in spite of life's storms. Every now and then a show or movie will accurately capture this (for example, movies such as *Juno* and *I Am Sam* or TV shows such as *This Is Us*, *Parenthood*, or *The Fosters*). Mostly, however, we are true-love starved.

Saying "I Love You"

I know personally how important it is to hear "I love you" from a parent. While I was growing up, my mom and I had a deep, nurturing relationship filled with love and acceptance. She was the one to whom I turned when I felt lonely, needed an attaboy, or needed an answer to a big question. She was the one who told me about the opposite sex and, later, what I should and shouldn't do with all the changes in my body. Hers was the lap in which I buried my tear-soaked face when kids at school made fun of me and accused me of horrible things that weren't true. She came to my basketball games, and when I was three, she decided that she needed to get me into church. She and I had a deep, loving relationship throughout my childhood.

Not so with my dad. In fact, we spent most of my childhood at complete odds. This only intensified when I became a teenager. It wasn't that my dad didn't want to love my sister or me; he just had a funny way of showing it. He was always angry, often explosively. We rarely heard positive words from him, and we never heard encouragement or approval in his tone. He had a gift for stringing multiple curse words together into a full-blown medley of explicitness. My sister and I were always on guard, vigilant for unpredictable outbursts.

In summers, when Dad was at work, we frolicked around our house from morning to afternoon, as free as young kids should be, without fear of scorn or shame. We romped with

Parenting for the Win

neighbor kids through the woods behind our house, built blanket forts in the living room, created imaginary worlds in our storage shed, and much more.

Until four thirty. When the short hand was just past four and the long hand hit six, everything changed. It had to. Dad would be home from work in sixty minutes. Everything we had done during the day had to be undone. Every beautiful imaginary world we had created had to be torn down and put back the way we found it. Every tool, every scrap of wood, every blanket or pillow had to be put back in its proper place, or we were in for it. From four thirty until five thirty every day we scoured the house, around the pond, the shed, and out by the street for anything that didn't belong. Most of our friends would evacuate long before Dad's arrival, but even if they were still hanging around, Dad was sure to rant and lecture and criticize despite our embarrassment.

Every now and then though something magical happened. The clock struck five thirty—and no Dad. A few minutes later, if he still had not shown, our hearts began to hope. *Could he have gone to the bar with the crew?* That would buy us at least three more hours. When the clock struck six, we knew. He wasn't coming home until late. By then we would be fast asleep, safe.

I hate every single word I just wrote because the truth hurts so deeply. I remember, even when I was just six or seven years old, vowing never to be that kind of father to my children. I hated the fear I felt when, in the middle of a day filled with imagination and wonder, I looked up and saw that it was four thirty. I hated the conflicting feelings I experienced—relief when he stayed out late, yet wishing I had my dad around.

This is no way for any child to live. And yet so many people have parents like mine. I knew my dad loved me, and he did many good things as a parent, but I was often left wondering if I was an inconvenience. Those formative years undermined my confidence, and I questioned my ability to stand up for myself. I doubted whether I would ever be good enough, whether my life mattered.

I'm not saying that Dad's presence or affirming words would have completely resolved my inner conflicts. But hearing "I love you, you are good enough, you matter" would have made a huge difference. I know many parents who have done child raising right. They accept their children's imperfections. They celebrate who their children are—their creativity, their messiness, their uniqueness—with no unjust criticism or judgment. And their children live free and confident in who they are. I did have several moments of affirmation growing up. I only wish it were not under the cloud of worry that I would be in trouble when my dad got home from work.

Of course, children should have to clean up their messes after playing, and they should respect the personal property of others. My dad wasn't wrong in enforcing these expectations. But he didn't stop to notice our creativity, nor did he express love for us—only shame. A healthy approach would have been first to marvel at our wondrous creation and then gently remind us to clean up.

I don't hold this against my dad. I have forgiven him, and I'm grateful that, especially in the past ten years, we have forged a deep, loving relationship. In fact, a recent experience with him highlights the importance of a parent's love. I'll never forget the summer of 2013. I was working in a large church on the north side of Indianapolis and was scheduled to speak one Sunday morning in all three main services. My mom and dad made the drive up from Cincinnati. They had only done that two times previously, so I was excited. And nervous. I remember seeing their silhouettes in the fourth row as I delivered the message. The service went well, and they came back to our house for lunch. Afterward, my dad was showing me his new Ford Explorer when he stopped in his tracks and looked me straight in the eye. "That was a really great service, Michael," he said. "You did a really good job with that sermon."

"Thanks," I said.

Then he said something I'll hold in my heart forever: "As I watched you, I thought, *That's my son up there.* I'm so proud of you!" And he hugged me.

I thanked him and wiped tears from my eyes.

Showing "I Love You"

Loving words are vitally important, but words alone are not enough. We have to reinforce our words with actions. So we must not only say "I love you" but also show "I love you."

I remember moments when my dad loved us through actions. On some summer nights, when my mom worked late, Dad would take us boating. Once, while driving to work, he heard a radio ad for a local amusement park and decided to take the day off, come home, and take his whole family for a day of adventure. And when my Little League coach benched me for too many errors, my dad was there with a hand on my shoulder while I cried. He didn't say anything, but he was there.

Words become cheap when they are not reinforced with actions. Yet actions can be empty when they are not accompanied by loving words. Parents, your words and actions combined have the power to build your children's confidence and self-worth higher and stronger than the tallest skyscraper in the world. And it is never too late. But please don't wait, and please don't hold back because it feels awkward. Build up your children. Cherish them. Fiercely defend them. Stand and marvel at their uniqueness.

Love them no matter what.

Love with No Strings Attached

Parents, do you love your children unconditionally, with no strings attached, even when they make mistakes or choose a path opposite of your hopes or expectations?

It may be obvious that we *should* love unconditionally, but *do* we? Do we keep on loving, in both word and action, when everything goes wrong with our ideal Gilmore Girl Dreamer vision, our perfect plan? Maybe our children fit perfectly into the plan we had when they first came into our lives. But I'm willing to bet, since they are freethinking, free-believing human beings, this is no longer the case. My goal in this chapter is to challenge one mistaken view of love.

Over all the years I worked in family ministry and later as a family consultant, I met hundreds of parents who loved their children—with strings attached. I knew it almost immediately when they began talking because their focus was entirely on their child's performance—what they did and didn't do or how they fell short of their parents' expectations. I never questioned a parent's love, but I often questioned whether their love came with conditions.

I'm not excusing a child's bad choices or an adult's permissive parenting. Household rules and boundaries are a must, and a child who isn't given healthy boundaries is in danger of a sense of entitlement, a lack of responsibility, and other issues that become harmful to their souls. Kristin and I don't tolerate disrespect, and we have enforced the truth that each of our kids must live with the repercussions of their choices, both good and bad. Unconditional love is not a get-out-of-jail-free card. But do boundaries and consequences need to overshadow parents' love for their child? I don't think so.

You can enforce a consequence or allow your child to suffer the repercussions of poor choices and still exercise unconditional love. The reason we often fail at loving unconditionally is that we allow our own vision, ideal, or plan for our child to trump our love for them. And we justify our conditions with all kinds of cover-ups.

What if we take on an attitude of love in our words and our actions, even when our kids find themselves in serious trouble?

What if we mix correcting, instructing, or teaching with gentle, affectionate affirmation that is fully supported by what we say and do? Can't we blend firm discipline with genuine love?

What if compassion and celebration of our kids lead the way instead of frustration over a mess to clean up? What if we gently remind them of their responsibility to clean up their messes while still delighting in their worth and creativity?

Kristin and I have adopted several children who suffer from fetal alcohol spectrum disorder. They have suffered permanent brain damage due to their pregnant birth mothers' alcohol consumption, hampering their ability to reason and control impulses. One of our kids reacts aggressively and impulsively, making parenting exhausting and defeating, especially when we don't have time to answer questions to his liking and his behavior escalates. We have had to learn to pay close attention to our words and our actions. Because of his prior trauma, harsh words tend to trigger even more out-of-control behavior. If our actions are defensive or abrupt, he tends to become defensive or abrupt. Many of our past, drawn-out battles with him could have ended much sooner had we kept our emotions in check. We have learned to remain calm in our tone and body language but still firm in our expectations.

A few years ago, our son threw a major temper tantrum at Christmastime. His brothers and sisters had already gone to bed, but he was still up, demanding TV time, his fifth snack, a twentieth glass of water, and more. At 10:00 p.m. the answer was "No, you've already had everything you need." His response was to grab keepsake ornaments off our Christmas tree and throw them against the wall. Merry Christmas to all, and to all a good night, right? He seemed to intentionally ignore the inexpensive Walmart decorations and go straight for the heirloom ornaments passed down five generations!

I was sitting at the dining table with my computer in front of me. My anger was like molten lava, and I was about to explode in an attempt to scare him out of ever doing such a thing again. Just as I stood to launch into my tirade, my screen glowed with an iMessage notification from Kristin, who was sitting nearby working on her own laptop. I glanced down and read, "Don't react to this behavior. There's nothing he can break that we can't replace or that has any meaning."

Yeah right, I thought. *What about Granny's heirloom ornament?*

Her message continued: "We can't give this behavior any attention. He wants us to react, but we can't."

I sat back down, focused on my laptop, and ignored what my son was doing just a few feet away. To this day, that's one of the toughest things I have ever done as a parent. Everything in me cried out to react, stop this behavior in its tracks, and make clear we would not tolerate it.

Then something amazing happened. Only a few minutes after my wife's insightful text, my son stopped what he was doing. Out of the corner of my eye I could see his shoulders drop and his body relax. When we could tell his tantrum was finished, Kristin and I calmly told him we were glad he chose to stop. Then we enforced the reality that he had to clean up the mess and return everything to its place. Our strategy worked.

Ponder this. What if, instead of immediately reacting in anger or frustration, we stayed calm? What if, instead of giving attention to bad behaviors and possibly escalating the situation, we patiently waited them out, and then firmly outlined the boundaries and consequences? How differently would our children react? How differently would tense situations turn out? And beyond this, what would we communicate to our children about how we feel about them, even if their choices and behaviors aren't what we desire?

That night, we didn't excuse bad behavior, nor did we belittle or shame. We simply waited. This strategy is commonly taught to parents who have adopted traumatized children, but I believe "calm and firm" is applicable to all parents. A parent's tone, reaction, words, and actions can make the difference between escalated behavior and peace. They can also make a difference in how our children see themselves and what they think we believe about them.

I'll give you another example. Every fall, my friends Jason Morriss and Andrew Schneidler and I lead a national event called Road Trip, exclusively for foster and adoptive dads (like the three of us). We take the guys up into the Colorado mountains for three days of conversation about life, parenting, failures, grace, fears, and more. We converse during meals, impromptu trips to microbreweries, mountain hikes, and nightly campfires. The time we spend together is beyond amazing, and if you are jealous, you should be. Jason leads the primary conversations during breakfast and dinner. This past fall, he asked a question that made me think about this chapter: "When my daughter has blown it, missed her period, and is scared of my reaction, will she feel safe coming to me, her daddy, and telling me what's going on?" He paused. "The role I take—judge or observer—determines the answer. Will I first defend her heart or point out her failures?"

The room full of normally boisterous men went silent. For the first time in many of those men's lives, they came face-to-face with a reality they had never considered: *Do I love my children no matter what?* Many of us were dealing with children from traumatic backgrounds, which often shattered our once-idealized pictures of life and parenting. We were at a crossroads, contemplating whether to accept and move into our new normal or continue to wallow in the loss of our Gilmore Girls parenting dream.

Do your children know you for your predictable lectures, orders, shaming, scorn, and overreactions?

Or do they know you for your grace? Your love? Your acceptance, no matter what?

The Other Side of Love

In Hollywood, love is romance. It's lovers embracing as the breeze blows through curtains and the moonlight pours in, spilling eerily across the floor. Hollywood sums up parental love in thirty- or sixty-minute episodes. It may be portrayed as tough, but resolution comes quickly.

Different aspects of genuine love are evidenced in the many words used to describe it: *sex, romance, infatuation, goose bumps, warm fuzzies, passion, belief, encouragement, commitment.* I want to suggest another important word to describe genuine love: *mess.*

What? Yes, messiness is an important part of true love. Love is the imperfection of living in these human bodies with these human thoughts and feelings that far too often betray us. It's figuring out how to pick ourselves up off the floor and move forward. Love is holding your child in your arms when she's so depressed she thinks about sneaking up to the medicine cabinet in the middle of the night and taking all the medications at once. And love does not shame her for this.

When your daughter comes home and tells you she's pregnant with no commitment to the father, no plan, and no way to care for a baby, love is looking her squarely in the face and saying you still love her deeply in spite of her choice (and that you love the child she's about to bring into the world, no matter what). Love still allows you to shut the door behind her and her petrified boyfriend as they leave and run up to your room to scream, cuss, and throw things for the next two hours because you are broken. Love is believing in her—that she's good and capable of hope and a future and of making responsible, wise choices—even when your expectations aren't met. Love is throwing your expectations out the window altogether but continuing to pray for her and hold on to hope for her.

Love is flying across the country to visit your son in a residential treatment facility after he became violent, unsafe, and unhealthy at home, victimizing his younger brothers and sisters. Love is spending a beautiful weekend with him in complete peace, and then having to drive away, leaving him sobbing on the facility's front step. Love is telling him he can't come home until he's healthy. Love is fighting for his heart and affirming him in spite of his past. Love is believing he also has hope and a future.

Love is hardwired so deeply within you that you would lay down your life for your children, bleed yourself dry for them regardless of their choices or the people they become. This is love. Yes, love is also romantic, passionate, happy, and carefree. Love is gathering around a Christmas tree with your family and singing carols. Love is breaking bread around the table and laughing as you reminisce about hilarious family vacations and awkward moments. Love *is* the goose bumps, the warm fuzzies. But these are just a few pixels in the bigger portrait of love. Love is a deep, determined attitude that remains even when the walls collapse or the fight intensifies or the hope fades.

So ask yourself, Do I love my child this way? Do I believe in them no matter what, no matter who they become? Do I love them as much when they screw up as when they don't?

Or are your preconceived notions, ideals, visions, and perfectly laid-out plans getting in the way of truly seeing your child and their heart? Are you more concerned with proving a point, winning an argument, or teaching a lesson than capturing their heart? Because I can tell you this: the true test of love is not when the road rises to meet you, or your child performs the way you hoped. The true test is when everything falls apart—your best-laid plans are a pile of ash and you are fighting to find any ray of light in the darkness. Can you continue to love your child more deeply than ever? Can you love your child as deeply in chaos as when you are in a place of peace?

The Lesson of Forgiveness

What about when we blow it with our kid? What about those times when we mess up, lose our temper, say something we don't mean, raise our voice unnecessarily, or completely lose our cool with our child—or even our entire family? Let's be honest here. It's not a matter of *if*; it's a matter of *when*. Because we are human beings. We make mistakes. We would like to say we've grown past this, but we haven't. I'm pointing at myself too.

A parent of influence bypasses the temptation to be a BFF to their children, focusing only on what makes them happy. A parent of influence steps out of the role of Dreamer, which is so wrapped up in an idealistic picture as to miss opportunities at hand, to truly lead. A parent of influence abandons the Commander approach, surrendering the insatiable longing to control, contain, or dictate. A parent of influence sidesteps the Instructor mode, standing in loving observation of their child before teaching a lesson. This is the secret sauce of winning the heart.

But what about those moments when we fail, when we lapse into one of these less-than-helpful default modes?

Can we seek forgiveness from our kids? And can we accept it from them? One of the most difficult things I've had to do is seek my child's forgiveness. It goes against everything in me, mainly because of pride and resistance to being vulnerable in front of my kid. But what is the cost when I don't let go of my pride and make things right? It's too high to risk. In my sixteen years on the parenting journey, I've learned what I must do to win my children's hearts.

As far as I've come, I still have far to go. Can you identify with me? We are going to fail sometimes. I recently took my three youngest sons camping. We had an amazing time together. But at the end of the weekend, my youngest son began to defy everything I asked him to do. My response was to scorn and lecture him. Finally, I lost my temper. Parenting fail!

I had to humble myself and ask his forgiveness. It was tough but so worth it. There is power and freedom in seeking forgiveness. It teaches our children how to forgive.

A few years ago, I lost my temper with my third-oldest daughter, who was thirteen at the time. She and I disagreed on something, and it escalated into a standoff and then a full-blown yelling match. Her tone was disrespectful, belligerent, and mean-spirited—completely inappropriate. I knew that I could dial down the fight by withdrawing as a combatant and ceasing to argue back. But it was one of those moments on my journey when I lost my way. I was consumed with winning the argument and had lost sight of her heart; I was no longer listening. Granted, her behavior was not acceptable. But I was the adult, the parent. I should have maintained control of my emotions. Rather than calmly and patiently listening, observing, and talking things out, I resorted to saying hurtful things to gain control and win. Regret instantly filled me.

My daughter burst into tears and darted upstairs to her room, slamming the door behind her. Embarrassed and angry with myself, I walked out to my car and drove away. I spent the next three hours at a nearby pub, watching football and trying to figure out what to do. I sent a text to Kristin and asked her how our daughter was doing. She had been grocery shopping, so she missed the spectacle. She replied, "She's sad and confused." I felt an inch tall. I asked her advice, and she said, "Give it until tomorrow and then seek her forgiveness. That's the only thing you can do." She was right.

I had a choice: I could wallow in self-pity and remain defeated, believing the voice that kept calling me a failure. Or I could swallow my pride and proactively make it right with my child. Two options, but only one was right.

At this juncture, many of us add to our mistakes. When we fail our children or our spouses, we often convince ourselves that we are failures and will never be any better. We allow our mistakes to define us. Then we give up and become content with the permanent identity of a loser.

But this line of thinking couldn't be further from the truth. Our mistakes do not define us. Failure is not your name or mine. Shame is not our identity. The best thing we can do when we mess up is to own it, make it right, and work on doing things differently as we move forward. It was hard, but that's exactly what I did the next morning. When my daughter came downstairs for school, I pulled her onto my lap, looked her in the eye, owned my mistake, and asked her forgiveness. She said nothing, only nodded. But that was that. There was nothing more to say. I did not need to defend myself or rehash the night before. I didn't even expect an apology from her for the things she had said. That may bother you, but I knew the target: winning her heart, not the argument.

My willingness to humble myself and win her heart bore unexpected fruit. A few days later, I was telling a friend about the incident, and he said, "So you sought her forgiveness?" "Yes," I answered. "It was hard, but I took my wife's advice." He thought for a second, then said, "You just modeled for your daughter how to forgive others. When she sees her daddy willing to seek forgiveness for his mistakes, it teaches her a valuable lesson and shows her where your heart truly is."

I was stunned. I had never thought of that. Seeking forgiveness, to me, traditionally meant admitting weakness. For years I had avoided it. My pride had always won out, especially in parenting. I had to be right, prove my point, and make sure my kids knew who was boss. But seeking my daughter's forgiveness was right. There was still much to repair in our relationship, and trust had to be earned back, but there was peace.

One of the beautiful payoffs from this instance (and many like it) is watching my children do likewise and seek others' forgiveness. Recently, when my daughter had participated in gossip about another kid in our neighborhood, she went to his house of her own accord, knocked on the front door, and apologized to him for her actions. My heart was warmed.

My friend was right, and his words opened my eyes. Loving our children means letting pride fall, admitting when we're wrong, seeking their forgiveness, and learning to live in a healthier manner. Doing so models to them how to forgive others. But I want to add one more thought. When we actively seek our children's forgiveness we model for them not only how to seek forgiveness but also how important it is to do so when we've wronged someone. And what better model is there than their parent? That's a powerful and transformative element of influence.

Pause to Reflect

1. How have you traditionally defined love?

2. How has your perspective on love dictated how you relate to your children?

3. What conditions do you find yourself placing on your love for your kids? What will it take to remove those conditions and love no matter what? (What messes are you willing to live with?)

4. How open are you to seeking your kids' forgiveness? If appropriate, plan how you will do this for a past or present wrong you've committed against your child.

12

A Parent's Greatest Enemy

Key 8: Listen to What Is True about You

If I were to walk down any street in the world and ask parents what they believe is their greatest enemy in parenting, what do you think they would say?

My children's behavior

Pop culture and its influence on teens

Negative music and movies

Drugs and alcohol

Pornography

Public schools

Fashion trends and battles over the clothes my kids choose

What if none of these are actual enemies of parenting? What if we've been accusing and fighting the wrong influences? I pose these questions because as I work to become a good parent, I've discovered my greatest enemy. It's fear. And I've found that fear presents itself in two big ways.

Fear of Inadequacy

I've explained that I grew up with a father who was explosive and would focus on the one thing I did wrong, even if I did twenty-five things right. It left me with a feeling of inadequacy in just about everything I did, even into my adult life. Anytime I achieved something great, I immediately began to think that I wasn't good enough or that others were better. These feelings of inadequacy plagued me well into my marriage and parenting years. It's precisely the reason I say that not only our encouraging words but also our blatant celebration of our children—in good and bad circumstances—are critical to their self-esteem and confidence.

I felt so inadequate that I used to wonder why my wife chose me as her husband. I believed that many other guys would have been better for her. In our early disagreements, I would say foolish things such as "Well, I guess you should have married _____ because he would be the person I'm not."

As you can imagine, this did not help. For years my own self-doubt and insecurities drove a wedge between us. Kristin believed she had to continually prove to me that I was good enough for her, and I thought I was continually proving that I wasn't. Feeling as though we constantly have to prove something to our partner is toxic to a marriage, and it took me years to conquer. Finally, Kristin looked me squarely in the eyes and told me to knock it off. She said she chose me because she *wanted* to be married to me.

I would like to say it ended there, but when I became a parent, my sense of inadequacy intensified. Maybe my interactions with my wife leveled out, but children gave me more reasons to feel inadequate. If my child was angry about something or frustrated with me, I took it as a sign that I wasn't a good parent. If they were moody and closed off or focused on something other than me, I gave full run to my sense of shortcoming. I spent years believing that behavioral issues related to our children's trauma before we adopted them somehow resulted from my bad parenting. Every meltdown, blowup, or problem at school was *my* fault.

My feelings of inadequacy hampered a genuine relationship with my children for many years.

One other common way the voice of inadequacy finds its way into our hearts is through the comparison trap. We see other parents who seem to have it all together, and we immediately begin comparing ourselves with them. Their children look happy, but ours always seem cranky, angry, and sad. They seem put together and organized while we feel lost and disillusioned. They seem to have an unending supply of energy for extracurricular events, but we yawn just thinking about doing anything beyond the minimum necessary for survival. We compare, we size ourselves up, and we fall short in our own eyes. We determine that we don't measure up as parents or spouses because we don't have what others have, or dress as they do, or provide as they do.

That's the fear of inadequacy working overtime to convince us we'll never be good enough.

Fear of Failure

Closely related to the fear of inadequacy is the fear of failure. In fact, it may actually be the evil dictator with the fear of inadequacy its first lieutenant. As a parent, I feared failing nearly every day. And when I was at odds with my children or said or did something that failed them, I believed I had lost them. I believed I would never be any better than my failures. It was an awful feeling, one of my greatest challenges on this journey. In the past, my fear of failing consumed and nearly crippled me, rendering me ineffective as a parent.

Fear of failure loves to insert itself in everything we do. Even when we are experiencing peace and connection with our children, fear of failure shows up and causes us to believe that the failure we've feared is a reality. It convinces us that our normal human mistakes are our complete undoing.

So when our teenager doesn't like us because we said no to something dangerous or unhealthy, we believe we've failed. We convince ourselves that their happiness or unhappiness is a direct result of our parenting success or failure.

Sometimes out of guilt over past failures and against our better judgment, we give in to begging. But we know we haven't done the responsible thing for our child, so we carry the weight of yet another failure. Not long ago, one of my teenage daughters pulled this nonsense, and I caved. Afterward, I beat myself up emotionally and mentally until my friend Jason spoke the blunt truth: "Stop thinking that way about yourself, Mike. You are no good for your kid or your family when you believe you've failed because of a small mishap on your part. It's not a reflection of your identity or worth as a parent. So stop it."

I hated to hear these words at first, but I needed to hear them.

The Mastermind of Fear

How does fear accomplish such defeat in our lives? Fear sabotages our inner voice and uses it against us. We so easily believe the things we hear in our minds. You know that voice. It whispers, *You are not good enough*, or, *Your kids deserve better*, or, *Your children wish they had someone else as a parent*, or, *You are the reason your children struggle.* We believe these and many other false messages because we hear our own voice speaking.

As a person of faith, I believe fear is one of many tools that Satan, the enemy of mankind, uses against us. And trust me, the enemy loves to convince me that I *am* inadequate and I *am* a failure as a parent, husband, and friend. When I believe this and give in to it, he wins. Fear wins, and I stay down. I don't get back up and continue forward. When I believe I'm a failure, I create a deep divide between my children and myself. When I believe I'm inadequate, I damage my relationships with my family members. My dim view of myself encourages in them a dim view of themselves. When I believe the lies of the enemy, Satan, who uses fear as a weapon to attack me, I'm rendered ineffective. I allow the space between my children and me to fill with guilt and resentment instead of apologies, silence instead of affirmation. When I give in to fear, it thwarts my opportunities to nurture, defend, lead, and model grace to them.

Have you been here? Knocked down by the fears of inadequacy and failure? Have you found yourself at odds with your children or spouse because you've given these fears undue power? If so, you are believing lies about yourself. You've allowed the enemy of mankind to win. And the precious ones who call you Daddy or Mommy pay the greatest price. The truth is, my friend, there is a heavenly Father who is greater than all your fears, and he has equipped you for adequate faithfulness and success with your family. And he's deeply and madly in love with you, so don't let your fears intimidate you. They can't keep you from being the best you can be for your family—not if you don't let them.

The Voice of Truth

You are *not* a failure. And you are *not* inadequate as a parent. Your children are *not* better off with someone else. Neither is your spouse. Your faithful efforts are *not* screwing up your kids or deepening their insecurities. But letting your insecurities dictate your interactions and relationships with them *might* screw them up.

And about the comparison trap: *be you.* Be happy that you are Mom or Dad to your kids. No one else in this world is called to be their parent. You are! Stop comparing yourself to others, no matter how perfect they might seem. The fact is you have no idea what goes on in their home or their life. You can't base your worth on what you don't know about someone else. Besides, your task in your family is not the same as my task or another parent's task in their family. Each family has its own challenges, and these can't be compared. I might be doing great at my assignment, even with little outward evidence.

You make mistakes, like everyone else, but those mistakes do not define you. So don't let them rob your children of the encouragement, empowerment, and confidence they so desperately need from you. When you give in to the narrative you hear playing in your mind and allow your mistakes to define you, in the long run your children begin to discredit your influence. Your fears don't change your opportunities or your power of influence.

You are a good mom. You are a good dad. Start listening to the voice of truth. We are under serious attack at all times. We exist in a world that bombards us with many voices, telling us to do this or that, follow this person, love like that mom, provide like that dad. But listen to what is true.

For years, I battled the voice of fear, convinced I was inadequate and a failure. And I stayed down. But finally, I learned to pray, *Lord, may the voice of truth speaker louder than the voice of fear.* When you pray that type of prayer, the voice of fear starts screaming. The attacks worsen. But the more you press into the truth about God and you, the more distant the other voice becomes. You'll still have days of insecurity. But even then you will become more confident in discerning what is true and what is not.

Keep Moving Forward

Recently, my son and I watched the 2007 movie *Meet the Robinsons*. It's a beautiful, inspiring, encouraging movie. My favorite scene is when Lewis tries to fix the broken time machine that brought him and Wilbur into the future. Lewis laments, "I don't even know what I'm doing!"

"Keep moving forward," Wilbur reminds him.

"I mean this stuff is way too advanced for me."

"Keep moving forward."

"And what if I can't fix this, what are we gonna do?"

"Keep moving forward!"

Wilbur explains that "Keep moving forward" became his dad's motto after he started Robinson Industries to mass-produce his inventions. One night, he woke up with the idea for a time machine. His prototypes failed 952 times! "But," Wilbur says, "he doesn't give up! He keeps working and working until he gets it right."

My next-favorite scene is when Lewis's gun explodes all over the family, and they celebrate his failure. As they all congratulate him on his failed attempt, Billie Robinson says, "From failure you learn. From success . . . not so much."[1]

Failures will happen, but they present us with a choice: either we stay down and wallow, or we get back up and *keep moving forward*.

This will be a fight, but it's worth your child's heart. They need you to make the right choice.

Pause to Reflect

1. How have you allowed fear of inadequacy or fear of failure to infiltrate your spirit and your parenting?

2. What has kept you from moving forward when you fail?

3. What are some steps you can take to resist the lying voice, listen to the truth, get back up, and move forward?

13

Potato Salad and Headstones

Key 9: Leave a Lasting Legacy

At conferences, I normally don't sit still for very long because of my severe ADD. Enduring long sessions is difficult, and I often miss much of what is said. This can make conference meals awkward when friends talk about something funny a speaker said, and I'm clueless.

There are, however, a few moments I distinctly remember from conferences over the years. Many years ago, I attended a seminar by leadership guru John Maxwell. It was centered on his then-new book, *The 21 Irrefutable Laws of Leadership*. He talked about legacy and what people will say about us after we die. At some point as he was speaking, I wrote down these words: "Shortly after you are dead and gone, people are going to stand around eating potato salad, and they are going to tell stories about you. They will start talking about your life. What you did with it and how you related

163

to the people you loved and the people you worked with. Ask yourself, 'What will they say about me?'"

I remember little else from that one-day conference. But that was all I needed. That was in 2000, eighteen years ago, but those words written in my notebook have stayed with me ever since.

Legacy.

As John Keating, played by Robin Williams, says in the movie *Dead Poets Society*: "We are food for worms, lads. Because one day we will stop breathing, turn cold, and die."[1] Truth! In that moment, what we do in life will either tell a positive, transformational story or will not. If we leave a legacy of love, kindness, grace, forgiveness, patience, self-control, and compassion, it will live on powerfully and positively through our children and their children and their children. It will go on to transform generations to come. Alternatively, if we are demanding, demeaning, controlled by our anger, or shaming toward our children, our legacy may be remembered but not in a positive light.

One way or another, our legacy will begin speaking through the memories people share at the gathering after our funeral when people are eating their potato salad. They'll be either laughing about the funny things we used to say or the crazy antics we pulled, fondly remembering tender moments with us, or wishing their relationship with us could have been different. This legacy, whether positive or negative, will outlive us in the way our children see and interact with the world. And it will help shape the way they parent their children. Do you see why the way you live your life now is so crucial to what happens after you are gone?

You and I will leave some kind of legacy. If it is a legacy of love, it will outlive us and continue to make a transformative impact. What will our life story say? Most importantly, what will our kids remember about us, their mother or father?

Inspired by a Headstone

Several years ago, when I was still a youth pastor, I ventured out with a camera crew to a local graveyard well off the beaten path to film a series of videos illustrating the significance of our life stories and what they tell the world. It was a frigid Indiana day just before Thanksgiving. The graveyard was hidden between cornfields, a stream, and a patch of woods. You wouldn't even know it was there unless you knew the area well. But it was well maintained. It had headstones from the late 1800s to present day. It is one of the most intriguing graveyards I have visited.

I had not previously paid much attention to headstones, other than those of people I knew, but here I began to look more closely. I noticed that most displayed a birth date and a death date. Then I found one that inspired me, belonging to a man named Charles who had been gone for thirty years. His inscription was a bit faded but legible:

"Papa Charles"
August 4, 1911–June 21, 1981
Loving husband
Devoted father
Faithful friend
Eternal dreamer
Christ follower
Your dash lives on through the lives you touched.

I have no idea who Papa Charles was, but on that cold afternoon I stood in wonder above his grave. I would never meet him this side of eternity, but I felt inspired by his life, perhaps more than by any other human being on earth. Apparently Charles lived a glorious life and left a lasting and meaningful legacy. The dash between his birth date and death date was alive even though he wasn't. That was his legacy, the story that outlived him. I'm willing to bet Charles did everything in his power, making the most of every moment he was given on earth, to ensure his dash would continue echoing into the future. "Your dash lives on through the lives you touched."

I would also like to think that in the days after Charles breathed his last, his loved ones, though saddened, began telling the story of his dash with joy and gratitude. I wish I could meet his children and hear the stories of their father. I long to hear how Charles lived, how he loved his kids, how he used his time, and how he viewed his influence. I don't think anyone receives the words on their headstone by happenstance. Words carved in stone are words with purpose.

We can't gather the man's entire story from one epitaph, but this final public testimony leads me to believe Charles fought hard to win the hearts of his wife and his children, and his investment will continue to earn eternal interest.

When my life is over, I hope my headstone tells a story similar to Charles's. With every ounce of strength I have, I want to live my life spending time with my kids, loving them unconditionally, and fighting hard for their hearts. I want my legacy to speak to these things.

Just Like Terry

I'll never forget the year 2004. I was serving as youth pastor in a small Indiana congregation. That year was my greatest test as a pastor and person of faith. Between August and November, our community tragically lost more than ten teenagers in car accidents. I labored on the front lines, counseling kids from my youth group who were grief stricken for their friends. Friends they had seen the day before as they left school for home. Friends with whom they had just danced the night away at homecoming. Friends who had slept over just days before breathing their last. I realized through this experience that no one is ever truly prepared for grief. And teenagers have no idea how to handle the emotions. As long as I live, I'll never forget sitting with other area youth pastors on our high school library floor with students who had collapsed in grief.

But that Christmas is even more deeply embedded in my memory. On the night of December 22, we received nearly eight inches of snow, and the next morning I awoke to a gorgeous winter wonderland. While my family slept, I slipped out to a coffee shop to finish a little work before wrapping up for the holiday. After an hour or two, I packed up my laptop and backpack and headed home through a crisp Indiana morning, eager to spend a day off with my family. I walked into the house, and Kristin met me with a concerned look. She had been crying.

"What's wrong?" I asked.

Shaking her head and looking down, she choked out, "Last night Abby and Adam's dad, Terry, passed away in his sleep."

167

I knew Terry from my work with a local before-school youth program. He was a good man. I was in shock.

A few minutes later, Kristin and I headed over to be with Abby, Adam, and their mother, Kristie. The atmosphere was somber as we gathered in their living room. Several of our students and youth volunteers were there comforting our friends; Abby and Adam were wrapped in their mother's arms. We prayed together for a long time. As we finished, Kristie pulled her kids close and said, "Your father loved you two so much. So very much!"

Later I learned that the previous night Abby, Adam, and a bunch of friends stayed up late with their father, watching TV and laughing at reality shows on MTV. What a great last memory.

A few days later, there was standing room only at Terry's visitation. Hundreds stood in line in the cold outside the funeral home for hours to pay their respects and hug the family. Both the visitation and funeral celebrated an extraordinary life.

As we drove away from the funeral, I thought, *I hope I live a life as extraordinary as Terry's.* At the time, I was a twenty-eight-year-old father with a long life ahead. I had three young children, and this experience caused me to refocus my attention and time. Terry's dash spoke. And today, Terry's legacy continues speaking through his children, who have both grown to be loving, kind, compassionate, and caring individuals.

I know my life and story will be unique, but if I have any influence in how my story is told or what my story looks like, I want it to be like Terry's. And I want a headstone that resembles that of Papa Charles.

How do you and I leave a legacy that speaks loud and long like Terry's? How can we be remembered like Charles?

Simple. We maximize the nine parenting keys to building a positive lifelong relationship with our kids.

A Look Back at the Nine Keys

This book is about recognizing and using our great influence in our children's lives. That's how we win their hearts and leave a lasting impression on them. We focus so much time and attention on insignificant things that we lose sight of what's important—our spouses and our children. These nine parenting keys are not the end-all, but they have changed the game for my family and are helping me become the best possible version of myself.

1. *Blend love and discipline for influence.* Begin by believing you are, in fact, a powerful and effective voice of influence in your child's life. Remember, your job is to be a parent, first and foremost. You are not just parenting for the here and now; you must think long term. Often, parents who fail to believe in their influence lose their way with their kids because they've forgotten their "why." The why is centered on love, healthy boundaries, and consistent parenting, regardless of the season.

2. *Understand and embrace The Shift.* When you suddenly realize you've dropped from first place of influence in your child's life to fourth place (behind their friends, culture, and other adults), what do you do? It's going to happen because your child is going to grow up, and your relationship will change. This child who used to tell

you everything and who wanted to spend every waking moment with you is suddenly distant and moody. First, remember you still have a voice in your child's life, but not the only voice. Second, embrace this change and progress with your child into new territory. If you resist it and fight for control, you'll default to a Commander or an Instructor. Or as a Dreamer you'll attempt to hold on to your idealized relationship, or you'll try to become their BFF. But these parenting styles run the risk of losing your child's heart.

3. *Amplify other voices of influence.* As they get older, your children are going to listen to other adults. They will gravitate toward others who care for them. Rather than resist, help select and champion healthy, responsible voices—small group leaders, pastors, teachers, coaches, trusted friends. Widen your child's circle with anyone who will tell your child the same things you have been saying but who will get a more receptive response.

4. *Use your time wisely.* You have been given a limited amount of time. To whom or what are you giving it? It belongs to the people who love you and call you Mommy, Daddy, husband, or wife. Our time can be divided and consumed by many meaningless competitors; we must reserve for our families our uninterrupted, undivided time. Work especially to seize the small, seemingly insignificant moments with your family and not just the bigger opportunities such as vacations. Take your child with you to the grocery store, throw a football to each other in the backyard, and so on. These add up to large quantities of quality time.

5. *Stay involved with your kids.* How involved are you in your children's lives? Remember, involvement is a gateway to personal, relational knowledge of your kids. Being fully present helps you learn and understand their likes, dislikes, dreams, fears, and struggles. Spend undistracted time with them, actively date them, and listen to their hearts.

6. *Commit to consistency.* Do you love your children consistently, particularly through regular time together? Do you set reasonable boundaries and enforce them with consistent consequences, so your children know your expectations? Do you stay awake to your children and what is happening in their lives? Are you consistently letting your children know how important their hearts are to you, especially by choosing to win their hearts and not just your arguments? Consistency is important to our children's health and to you. It builds trust, even when your consistent choices are unpopular, even when you have to guide them through life's hard times. Consistency equals maximum results.

7. *Love no matter what.* How do you respond when your child fails? Do you love, or do you lecture or shame? Do you love your children unconditionally, or do you withdraw your love when they don't meet certain conditions? Are they free to be who God created them to be, or are your expectations slowly suffocating them? And when you have failed them, do you seek their forgiveness or does pride win out? Love is far from easy—it can be messy—but it is always worth it.

8. *Listen to what is true about you.* The greatest enemy of parents is fear, which shows up in two ways—fear of

inadequacy and fear of failure. We easily believe that we are inadequate as parents, especially when we are caught in the comparison trap, holding ourselves up to other parents or to some worldly standard. This leaves us feeling we're less than we are. Fear of failure convinces us that our mistakes as parents and human beings define us. But grace changes all this. The grace that Jesus has willingly given us frees us from these two fears.

9. *Leave a lasting legacy.* When you are dead and gone, what will your children say about you? What story represents the dash between your birth and death dates? Did you love your children unconditionally? Did you model forgiveness and servanthood before them? Did you observe and marvel at their brilliance or point out their shortcomings? What kind of legacy will you someday leave?

This is just the beginning. You must continue the fight to win your children's hearts every day of their lives. It is not a one-and-done prospect. Keep wielding love and wisdom, even when it's extremely hard. Choose to love these amazing, beautiful people with whom you've been blessed. Celebrate your children's successes, and celebrate *them* through their failures. You will face seasons of doubt and disillusion and seasons of hope and fulfillment with your children. That is the tragedy and the beauty of the parenting journey. Stay the course.

Pause to Reflect

1. What kind of legacy are you leaving for your children?

2. How have you modeled the values you hope to pass on to your children?

3. What has hampered the quality or impact of your legacy, and what can you do to change the way things are?

4. What do you want your headstone to say?

PART 3

MOVING FORWARD

14

The Hats Parents Wear

Defining a Good Parent

Once you apply the nine parenting keys and begin healthily exercising your influence in your child's life, you will move into a new day. You will still face difficult seasons but with a clarified intention. You know what you are fighting for—your child's heart. You are learning to control your emotions, to stand in observation of your precious child.

I recently heard my son say to his younger brother words that we had made clear were never acceptable: "You're stupid." *Busted*.

I sat the offending brother down and made him look me in the eye. I could have come down hard on him. I could have shamed him, told him how bad he was for making this choice, scorned him for ignoring our frequent instruction. But at what cost? Did I want to be right, or did I want to connect with my son? Did I want to win the argument or capture his heart?

For many years, I did not understand wise parenting options. My default was "Serve your consequence, and that's final!" I made no effort to connect with my children. How often have we missed precious opportunities?

Thankfully, that day my head was on straight. My son had to suffer a consequence for using language that tears others down. But I took this opportunity to build my child up. He sat next to me, his eyes fixed on the ground, clearly regretting his words. I whispered his name. He slowly raised his gaze to my face. Our eyes met, and I calmly said, "Son, do you think it makes someone feel good or bad to hear those words spoken to them?"

He shook his head and murmured, "Bad."

"And would you want someone to say those words to you, or about you?"

He shook his head again.

"I don't want you to use those words again, buddy. You are better than words like that. You have a good heart in you, and the way you love people is amazing. Never forget that. You are a loving person, son. One of the most loving people I know. I'm proud of you for that!"

He thought about my words. Then he raised his head and smiled.

I want my boy to become a person who speaks kindly to others, a man of character and integrity. But that means I have to be a man who speaks kindly to others, including to him. I have to live with character and integrity. That's not always easy, especially when I've repeated something a billion and five times and I think I'll explode if I have to say it once more. But explosions do zero good for my children or for me. I know this from experience. I have worked to overcome my frustration, and the wiser approach becomes easier when I see the positive results of building up my children. I have learned that is what good parents do.

Parents in the Bible

Not long ago, I was at odds with one of my kids over several things. I of course stuck closely to my perspective, while she held on to hers with a death grip. Neither of us would budge. Sound familiar?

An acquaintance of mine, listening to my lament, offered some advice: "You need to take a look at biblical parenting. Get your answers there. What did parents in the Bible do?"

The Bible is chock-full of very, shall we say, *interesting* examples. It's not meant primarily as a parenting guide, though it does provide the essential wisdom parents need. Although Jesus and Paul provide many principles for parents—such as forgiveness, patience, and truthfulness—neither man was a parent, so we can't look to them as parenting models. But consider the following parenting examples from the Bible.

Noah. Solid example, right? Noah built an ark to save his family, trusted God even when it didn't make sense, and was affirmed by God as a pillar of faith. The Bible even says, "Noah did everything exactly as God had commanded him" (Gen. 6:22). His devotion to God must have served well as a model to his sons. But we see that Noah is less than perfect based on some events after the flood (Gen. 9:20–27).

Abraham. In Romans 4, Abraham is considered the spiritual father of all who live by the kind of faith he exemplified, and there are many good things to say about him as a parent. We might be bewildered at his willingness to sacrifice his son's life (Gen. 22:1–19), until we realize that it was against his will and in profound faith in the God who commanded the sacrifice. Still, the Hagar-and-Ishmael story arc demonstrates Abraham's imperfections (Gen. 16, 21).

Jacob. The nation of Israel was named after Jacob. Indeed, all twelve of his sons remained loyal to him until his death, and in Genesis 49 we see that he knew them well. However, some accused him of favoritism toward Joseph and Benjamin, the only two sons born of his dearly loved Rachel. So again, we have a good man who has his own share of faults.

Mary and Joseph. The young Mary accepted responsibility for bearing and raising the Messiah, even though it must have been a shock when she received this calling. Joseph also accepted a difficult role, raising a son who everyone knew wasn't his. We know they both loved Jesus and treated him with kindness—in spite of the fact that for three days they lost track of him after a family trip to Jerusalem (Luke 2:41–51). For those of us who are foster or adoptive parents, all we can think when we read this story is "Department of Child Services investigation!"

There is something I love deeply about these stories: all are about real parents who were real people who made mistakes, yet their mistakes did not disqualify them from being used in mighty and undeserved ways. That is the power of grace. I identify with that. I have blown it big-time in my sixteen years of parenting. I have said, thought, and done things that should disqualify me. But as we reminded the guys at this past year's Road Trip event: "You are good dads and husbands. Your past failures do not define you. You are defined by the One who deeply delights in you." As with Noah, Abraham, Jacob, Mary, and Joseph—all imperfect human beings—our shortcomings and sins do not define us. They are not our names. This is true also for grandparents, aunts, uncles, caretakers, guardians— anyone with responsibility for children's lives. Our perfect Parent delights in all of us imperfect parents. Grace changes everything.

You've made it this far in a book about parenting, which proves you want to be the best parent you can be and you want the best for your children. Being a good parent is not about being perfect or making all the right choices or never messing up. It's about accepting this great opportunity in spite of our imperfections. It's about leading with compassion, unconditional love, and grace because we have received these so abundantly ourselves.

The Bible does not present us with solid parenting examples—only real people like us. But it challenges us to bear the fruit of love, joy, peace, patience, kindness, goodness, faithfulness, gentleness, and self-control (Gal. 5:22–23). It instructs us to talk about the hope we have with our children from sunup to sundown (Deut. 6:7). It reminds us that forgiving others as we have been forgiven is the best possible way to live (Matt. 6:12). Thank God that he sees our hearts and not only our outward behavior (1 Sam. 16:7).

Four Roles of Good Parents

Let me spell out four roles, among others, that define a good parent.

Nurturers

I grew up believing my mom was the nurturer, the person to whom I looked for loving kindness and gentleness when I was broken, and my dad was the disciplinarian, the person to whom I looked for lessons in confidence, strength, and leadership. I ran to Mom when I was hurt or sad or crushed and to Dad when I needed advice or assistance. I carried this understanding into the first few years of my own parenting journey. When my very young children were upset, I backed away from them, thinking their mom was the one they wanted. I shied away from snuggling with them at bedtime or cuddling during family movie nights because I feared this would diminish their picture of me as the family's strong leader. And then I realized something—I love to nurture just as much as my wife does, and she loves to lead and teach just as much as I do.

Kristin and I both love all the parenting roles, whether they are "supposed" to be the mom's or the dad's. I think our society has bought into a lie. One of my favorite things is to care for my children when they are sick or hurting. Recently, I took my three youngest sons camping. My second youngest son woke up cold during the night, and his whimpering woke me up. When he told me what was wrong, I instantly climbed out of bed to help him readjust his bed and get warm again. I tucked him in and reassured him I was there to help him get warm. I wrapped my arms around him and held him close until he fell asleep. If I subscribed to traditional beliefs, I wouldn't have responded in this way. I might have told him to suck it up and stop crying. What good would that have done in that moment? Would that have deepened my connection with my son?

Likewise, my wife has spent the majority of our lives together as a stay-at-home mom, taking care of our home and our children. It's a bigger, more important job than I've ever had. She's a leader among leaders. She speaks eloquently and with confidence, never mincing words. Within our household, she takes the lead on many things and I'm happy to follow. Recently, when I was away from home for a few days, she not only kept our children moving through school schedules and extracurricular activities, but she also handled several household repairs and, by watching videos on YouTube, figured out a cheaper alternative to a problem with one of our cars, saving us a small fortune. And this was in one day! When we first moved out to our farm, we experienced power failure. She not only called the power company but also negotiated with them the cost of the project. She really is Superwoman! If she subscribed to traditional beliefs, she would wait for me to fix things (I'm terrible at this) or to take the lead in teaching our kids strength and courage. Again, would this accomplish anything good?

Moms and dads are both nurturers. Moms and dads are both leaders. Moms and dads are both models of courage and strength. Moms and dads can both wield a toolbox and google how to fix a furnace. (True story!) Don't believe that only moms are nurturers and only dads are fixers and leaders. When both parents embrace a nurturing role, kids attain greater self-confidence and security.

Defenders

Being a defender is another trait that is not gender specific. We have this amazing privilege of standing in defense of our children. But what does this mean? When you hear the word *defense*, a few things come to mind. You might think of defense from physical danger. And certainly that's part of it, but there is so much more. Our kids live in a world that tries to convince them they are failures, less than worthy, and not good enough, pretty enough, smart enough, or talented enough. Good parents defend their children's hearts and defend what is true about their spirits, their brilliance, and their humanity. They defend them from the words of cruel classmates or an overly harsh coach. They defend them against a world that demands a certain look, dress code, status, or performance. This strengthens the parent-child bond.

Do you remember the 1992 movie *A League of Their Own*? If not, watch it as soon as possible. It's an American classic. The film chronicles the all-female professional baseball league that began during World War II. In an early scene, baseball scout Ernie Capadino travels with new recruits Kitt Keller and Dottie Hinson to see another prospect, Marla Hooch. She's a phenomenal baseball player who outslugs the boys. But when she lifts her cap, Ernie recoils; he's so repulsed by her unattractiveness that he dismisses her extraordinary baseball talent. He starts to walk away, but Marla's father confronts him and fiercely defends his daughter. He explains that he raised her to be like the boys, and he asks Ernie not to discount her.

This is what it means to defend our children. We fight for them when the world turns against them or looks down on them. We stand between the child we fiercely love and a world hell-bent on performance and appearance. This does not mean we storm into the principal's office and rescue our kid when they have set fire to the school or cheated on a test or stolen money. But we defend their worth, their talent, their creativity, and their value, which never diminish.

We can defend our kids when we truly see who they are. As my friend Jason says, "We must become seers of our kids in order to become their defenders." When we step back from being lecturers and controllers, we free up space to take on this crucial role of defender, which is one of our highest expressions of love and grace.

Our children's self-confidence, sense of value, and success depend on our fierce defense of the truth we see and know about them.

Leaders

I used to believe that my job was to fix my kids. Several of my kiddos were adopted out of trauma, which has caused behaviors and struggles that have sometimes made life difficult. But the majority of these behaviors are not their fault, though I used to think they were. Several years ago, I saw my children as bad kids behaving badly. I thought my primary role was to manage their behavior, to control it to the best of my ability. But I soon realized that was not my calling as their parent. In fact, we cannot force our kids to match our expectations. We can work to influence their hearts and their behaviors, but it's futile to attempt full control. And focusing only on externals—enforcing outward compliance to an external standard—without also addressing the heart creates kids who work harder simply not to get caught, rather than kids who take personal ownership of the value of good behavior. I had a father who tried to modify my behavior through yelling, lectures, and scorn. All I did was pay closer attention to outward detail so I wouldn't be caught next time.

What does it mean to lead? Among other aspects, a leader is a model, someone who leads by example, who lives out what they say. (Modeling is so important that I'll deal with it as a separate parenting role.)

A leader is a decision maker, someone who first listens patiently but who also takes appropriate responsibility when a decision is required.

A leader is one who boldly goes before others, who bravely steps out as a point man or point woman to stand in the gap between the danger ahead and the followers behind.

A leader not only enforces healthy standards and boundaries, as we've seen, but also lives by those standards with integrity. A person of integrity is the same in private as in public. Their outward actions can be trusted to reflect who they are inside.

A leader is also a servant. They put others first and see to their needs.

And a leader is respectful toward others. We as parents must respect our children in the same way we expect them to respect us and others in authority.

You are not called to control or contain or dictate. You are called to lead authentically. Maybe you have never thought of yourself as a leader, but let me assure you: regardless of gender, when you are a parent, you are a leader! In the middle of a battle with your child, it's critical to your relationship that you step back, maintain your emotions, and remember your role.

Models

We are to model grace, compassion, forgiveness, patience, kindness, gentleness, and self-control to our children. Even after The Shift, when we are suddenly moved to fourth place in the influence rankings, our preteen, junior high, or high school kid is taking life cues from us, even when they don't seem to be listening. I know it feels as though everyone else has more influence in our child's life, but rest assured that they look to us as models. They are trying to figure out how to live in and relate to a world gone mad. They are searching for identity, purpose, and a place in this world. Sure, they will take cues from their friends, and they will be influenced by celebrities. But at the end of the day they want to learn from us, their parents, even if they don't show it. We have this unique and glorious opportunity to model the most important values and life skills for our kids.

And the best part? When we do this effectively—when we put aside fear and insecurity and believe that we are influential in our child's life—we don't have to do nearly as much verbal teaching. Our children will see the virtues on display in our lives, and they will begin to apply what they see to their lives.

Parents Who Win Hearts

Some of my favorite on-screen parents are in the 2010 movie *Easy A*, the story of Olive, a high school girl who makes use of her school's rumor mill to advance her social and financial life. When she lies about her dating life, she finds herself in hot water. The dialogue between Olive and her parents throughout the film is comical, but I want to highlight the parents' patience and calm demeanor, no matter what Olive tells them. They illustrate the roles of nurturer, defender, leader, and model.

When Olive freaks out over something her best friend did to her, Olive's dad doesn't scorn, shame, shut her down, or tell her she's overreacting. He asks if she's okay. When Olive admits being sent to the principal's office for calling another student a vulgar name, her parents respond with patience and kindness first. Rather than immediately jumping to conclusions or handing down a consequence, they build a connection first. They give Olive an opportunity to explain, and they listen. Olive's parents believe she's a good kid, even though her choice of words wasn't okay. They know her heart and spirit because they have taken the time to learn about her. They also recognize a season in the relationship that looks different from previous seasons. They handle The Shift in a way more parents need to follow. We've done damage to our kids by our overreaction to situations that weren't the end of the world, all in attempts to dictate control or change mere external behavior. Certainly, we must set and enforce boundaries, but these should be done with kindness and compassion, never by beating our kids down.

Pause to Reflect

1. How have you allowed your past mistakes and short-comings to define you as a parent (or as a human being)?

2. List some ways you are a good parent. In what ways have you been a nurturer, defender, leader, and model to your children? (Celebrate your successes!)

3. How can you better fulfill one or more of the four roles of good parents?

15

Eyes on the Prize

Parenting Is a Long-Term Investment

I have never been particularly good at managing money. In fact, I've been awful at it. It's not that I'm a spendthrift, and I don't have a gambling addiction. I don't buy frivolous things or carry massive debt. Currently, my only loan is my mortgage. But I don't keep track of income and outflow very well. And I'm not good at balancing a checkbook.

I grew up with parents who saved money well. My dad retired early and enjoyed many years of financial freedom before any of his coworkers were able to retire. My mom also took early retirement after thirty years at her workplace. My dad was a wise investor, but neither of my parents taught my sister or me to save or invest.

All this changed in 2008, however, when Kristin and I went through Dave Ramsey's Financial Peace University at our church. We were drowning in debt at the time. One year into a home mortgage we couldn't afford, we also had credit card debt that was becoming unmanageable and two hefty car loans that hung over us daily like thick dark clouds. We had no joy and certainly no peace. It was stressful for our family and marriage. Over the next few years we were able to pay off much of our debt, refinance our mortgage with better terms, and learn about a foreign concept—investing.

On a warm spring afternoon in my early thirties, I met with a financial adviser who talked me through options such as IRAs, a 403b, high-growth mutual funds, stock options, and a retirement plan. I will never forget that meeting because, for the first time in my life, I understood the importance of thinking long term. I realized that I had to stop focusing solely on the present and think more in-depth about the future. *My* future. *Our* future. And more importantly, *our children's* future. How Kristin and I invested our money now had to be determined by the dividends it would pay out later. The financial adviser was very clear: if we began investing consistently today and over time—patient, undeterred if the market took a downturn, continually making deposits into our investment account—it would pay high dividends in the future when I reached retirement.

I learned a simple truth about financial investments: they take time to grow and mature. They don't reach their full growth potential in five, ten, or fifteen years. The longer we invest in them, the richer they become. Then, after thirty or forty years of consistency—staying at it even when the deposits are difficult to make—they pay big dividends.

Parenting our children is much like an investment. The relationship we hope to have with them in their adulthood takes time to grow. We don't get to take full advantage of the mature relationships when our children are adolescents. Fruitful friendships with our children are dividends that pay out once we have put in the long, hard years of parenting them with boundaries, consistency, and sometimes tough love.

Earlier I shared that everything I know about influence I learned from my mother-in-law. I described how, when my wife was growing up, her mother was not her best friend. Her mother was her parent. Yes, Kristin's mom seized valuable opportunities to have lunch, special coffee dates, and deep conversations with her that shaped and molded my wife into the strong woman she is today. But when Kristin crossed a boundary, my mother-in-law enforced it and imposed consequences. She didn't do this harshly, but she did it consistently. There was no mistaking who was in charge in their household. Ask Kristin about her childhood, and she will share fond memories. She will also tell you she was parented with consistency and love, even when the journey was long and hard for her parents and her relationship with them was shaky. That is what produced her strong friendship with her mother today. They weren't best friends when Kristin was a child or a teenager, when the relationship required her mother and father to parent her. But they are best friends now.

Interestingly, Kristin's mother and father retired well off financially. They also saw their parenting task as an investment. They made consistent deposits over time. They understood the value of investing over the long haul, both monetarily and relationally.

How, then, do we invest in our children in order to enjoy large relationship dividends with them in the future? If you are asking this question, you are on the right track already. Following are a few principles to help you formulate the right focus now, whether your children are elementary age or teens.

Time

Earlier I talked about the importance of investing a quantity of quality time in our children. Doing so embeds deep within them a sense of their value and your love for them. But now, with an eye to the endgame in the parenting journey, I want to look at another aspect of time. In keeping with the advice from my financial adviser, our "accounts" with our kids take time to grow. They won't reach full maturity in five years or even fifteen years. We must keep making contributions over the long haul in order to receive maximum dividends. And that takes great patience on our part.

When my daughter was born sixteen years ago, I began a journey that continues today. And over the next eight to ten years, well into her adult life, I will still be her parent. That never ends. But my relationship with her will evolve, and after a long time my investment will begin to reach its full potential. In order to maximize our investment and ensure the greatest future returns, we must remain faithfully committed to our children for a long time.

If your child is young, your investment period is just beginning and will continue for the next twenty-some years. You will endure many difficult days between now and the maturity of the relationship. In some seasons, your investment won't seem to grow, and everything you put into your child's life will seem meaningless. But even through The Shift and other tough times, your patient consistency will produce growth. You must keep your focus on the end result, the ultimate payout.

If you are parenting a teen and just waking up to the urgency, you have a shorter time to invest. But you can still get moving. Time is of the essence. Your baby is but a blink away from stepping out of the nest and into the real world, but you can still make a difference by investing lovingly and wisely in your child every day for many years to come.

Investing in our children takes great patience. In 2008, the US stock market crashed and the housing market plummeted. Many desperate Americans panicked and rushed to cash out their retirement funds. They couldn't see any hope of recovery and didn't want to lose more money. They were driven by emotion, not logic. But some investors had a different perspective and wisely counseled patience, leaving money right where it was, expecting the market to recover. Why? Because it had always recovered before. After each of the many downturns in US history, the market always came bounding back. Some even advised buying stocks during this time because they were cheap and would eventually grow. Those who followed this advice saw maximum growth just a few years later.

Unfortunately, we live in a culture that isn't very patient. We grow impatient waiting at Starbucks, in line at the grocery store, in construction zones, and even while on vacation in restaurants. As parents, we often give in to impatience even in regard to the long-term investment in our children. When our relationships with them take a downturn, we begin to panic and grow restless. Some begin to overparent or increase the severity of discipline, asserting Commander or Instructor authority in fear of losing control. Others become Dreamers or BFFs, desperately hoping that befriending their children is the answer.

The key is simple—remain patient. Keep on parenting your child with a healthy blend of discipline, intentionality, love, and guidance over the long haul.

Consistency

When investing in our children's lives, it's not enough simply to wait a long time and hope for good relationships with them. We must use the time well, consistently making healthy investments in their lives.

Consistency is a game changer for any investment. Remember the tortoise and the hare? The sole reason the tortoise won the race was his consistency. While the hare took a nap, the tortoise stayed the course. Our consistent investments of love, time, nurture, boundaries, and so on are especially important during the difficult seasons because those are the times when our children may be making hard choices. We may feel like a failure, but so do they. If we remain consistent through the difficult days and seasons, we will see results.

If it is late in your parenting journey and you are just now beginning to turn things around, it's going to be painful. I once decided to run a half marathon in Indianapolis. Even though I had trained for this race, it was tough. The first seven miles were excruciating. My body was in distress. Every step was painful. But my goal was to finish, and I kept going. I set my mind on the finish line, not on the pain in my legs and feet. Something amazing happened when I reached mile 7.5. I experienced the "runner's high." My body adjusted, and I suddenly felt as though I was running on air. I finished in good time and felt great. If I had given up in the first seven miles, I never would have reached the runner's high or the finish line.

Consistency in your parenting (and in all of life) is a game changer.

Keep Your Eyes on the Goal

Many parents ask, "If I invest in my children's lives for years, what should I expect in the future?" Every parent-child relationship is different. I've known many parents who struggled with their children through the adolescent years, but then maturity took over, reconciliation occurred, and their relationships became healthy. That's my story with my dad. After a difficult history, I now talk with him almost weekly, and we enjoy each other's company. I love my dad, and he loves me.

I've also seen a handful of parent-child relationships that were healthy through the child's adolescent and teen years but then took a downward turn. We can't predict the path of our relationships, just as we can't predict the stock market. There are many unknown factors between now and adulthood. However, I can tell you that I've seen many success stories with parents who chose to invest time, love, influence, boundaries, and more into their children's lives throughout their childhood. In particular, parents succeed when they understand and embrace The Shift; when they avoid the traps of Commander, Instructor, BFF, or Dreamer; and when they choose to be influential parents.

You probably hope for a healthy friendship with your children in their adult years, a peer-to-peer relationship with the babies you brought into the world, welcomed into your home, and raised to adulthood. As I've said, I've never met a parent who looked at their newborn baby or the child they just adopted and thought, *Gosh, I hope I screw this kid up!* We all want the end result to be the stuff of an Oscar-worthy film. We want to look back someday and think, *I did a good job!*

So we must keep our eyes focused on the future in everything we do with our children. Every single deposit in their hearts should be guided by the question, What do I want the end result to be? There is powerful truth in my wife's statement: "We're not raising children; we're raising adults!" It's hard to remember this on the dark days and to keep in mind that we shouldn't expect the ultimate returns too soon. They will come, but down the road. That's when the baby girl or boy we've raised will relate with us as a friend. This will occur only after we've consistently put in the time through the elementary years, through The Shift of the teen years, and into adulthood. Do not give up either love or loving discipline. Parenting with a forward view, day in and day out, is what will result in future rewards.

As I write this, I'm enjoying a weeklong vacation with my family in St. Petersburg, Florida. I'm writing early in the mornings while my family is sleeping. We needed this vacation! It was a long and brutal winter back home where, in fact, it's snowing right now, well into the spring. Here in Florida it's 80 degrees and sunny. My in-laws are also here, and Kristin and her mother have enjoyed many long talks as friends while doing laundry together or working in the kitchen. They tell each other everything. These are the rich dividends of a long-term investment.

The other night we were all together and talking about Kristin's childhood, and the subject turned to influence. Her

mom shared some funny stories about discipline and boundaries. She told of her decision to take Kristin out for coffee
consistently during Kristin's high school senior year because
her daughter would soon be leaving home for good. She took
the time to invest in her daughter before she stepped into
adulthood. Kristin shared how much she cherished those
times together.

The longer and more focused our investment in our children's lives, the greater the relationship dividends in the
future.

Pause to Reflect

1. Why is a long-term parenting viewpoint important?

2. Consider your parenting. What dividends do you hope to see in the future when your children are grown up?

3. What are you doing now to ensure that your investment in your children will pay richly in the future?

16

Direction Determines Destination

Parenting with More Than Good Intentions

I'm a big fan of the Ohio State University Buckeyes. I bleed scarlet and gray. I grew up outside of Cincinnati along the banks of the Ohio River in the small town of New Richmond, where rooting for Ohio State is almost a religion. My wife grew up in Westerville, Ohio, where the religion had grown to the point of hatred for the rival University of Michigan Wolverines. Game days were holy, and Woody Hayes sat not at the right hand of God but in close proximity. You may think I'm joking, but anyone from Ohio will affirm the seriousness of Buckeye fandom.

I love to load a car with friends decked in Buckeye colors early on a crisp fall Saturday morning and drive east on I-70 from Indianapolis to that beloved city, Columbus. A hundred thousand rabid fans converge on the mecca known as Ohio Stadium—aka the Horseshoe—to cheer ourselves hoarse for victory. There's nothing like it, and I try never to let a season go by without attending one of these spectacles. Nonfans have told me that being in Ohio Stadium on game day is beyond anything they have ever witnessed.

Suppose on one of those beautiful Saturday mornings I dressed up in my Buckeye jersey with my buck-nuts necklace around my neck and entered I-70 *westbound* toward St. Louis, Missouri. What would happen? I can tell you what *wouldn't* happen—I wouldn't make it to the Ohio State game because I would be driving the wrong direction. I might *wish* I was going the right direction. I might *hope* I was going the right direction. I could *say* I was going the right direction. I could even *pray* I was going the right direction.

But unless I exit I-70 westbound, turn around, and head back east, I will never reach my intended destination.

The Journey Is about Direction, Not Just Intention!

Author and pastor Andy Stanley shares what he calls the principle of the path: "Direction—not intention—determines destination."[1] I read this nearly eight years ago, and it still resonates with me. It applies to many aspects of life, especially parenting.

Consider how often in our lives we *intend* to do something—complete a home renovation, pay off consumer debt, take better care of our health, spend more time with extended family—but we don't. Why not? Likely because we're moving in the wrong direction. If our intention is to lose thirty pounds but we keep stopping by Starbucks or McDonald's, we're going the opposite direction of weight loss. If we want to eliminate consumer debt but we keep defaulting to credit instead of cash, we're going the opposite direction of financial freedom. In September 2016, I started a room addition to our house. My intended few days turned into weeks and then months. I *intended* to finish the room, but I wasn't moving in the right direction.

We can spend our hands-on parenting years intending to do all the right things with our children. But if we are not actively taking steps to move in that direction, we will never reach our intended destination. If my child continually crosses the household boundaries I've established, I must consistently enforce the consequences. If I hope to raise children of character, I must take steps to model character as an individual and in my family. If I want to have healthy friendships with my adult children, I must mark my destination now and consistently influence and guide them during their childhood and teen years. This is hard, especially when we fear we're losing our influence and are tempted to default to one of the four unhealthy parenting styles. But any of these—Dreamer, BFF, Commander, and Instructor—will derail us and lead us away from our intended destination. These modes of parenting are usually littered with good intentions, but they lack valid direction.

We easily fall into a pattern of having good intentions but not following through. Recently, my sixteen-year-old daughter reminded me that when she was four I had promised to take her and her older sister on a hot air balloon ride. It was a hot summer day, and we had spotted a balloon in the distance. Excited, I loaded the girls and their younger brother into our minivan, and we had chased it down. A few miles from our home, sitting in a church parking lot, we watched the aircraft float through the still, steamy Midwest sky. I held my girls on my knees and whispered my promise.

Fourteen years later, it remains unfulfilled. My intentions were good, honorable, and loving. But I had not taken steps in the right direction.

The depth of our parental influence is determined by the direction of our actual movement as individuals and with our children. Remember that. It's too easy to start with loving intentions but become lax in our convictions, values, and promises. We live in a time when the abandonment of values and promises is now as common as breathing. Just look at the divorce rates in the United States, for example. More than 40 percent of marriages end in divorce.[2] Those couples intended to stay married when they walked down the aisle, but they lacked the direction needed to stay true to their promise. You see much the same in college dropout rates and many meaningless career changes. No wonder genuine movement in the right direction has become such a struggle for parents.

We Can't Lead Where We Are Not Going

We've talked about the importance of boundaries for our children. But what about boundaries for us, their parents? The fact is we can't lead where we are not going ourselves. Neither can we influence them with anything that isn't influencing us. If we intend to lead our children in a specific direction, but we aren't moving in that direction ourselves, our leadership and influence are meaningless.

Long ago I heard from my parents: "Do as I say, not as I do!" You may have heard this from your parents. Let me interpret: "I am the parent. I'm in charge. You are the child. You are not in charge. I'm telling you to do something, and it doesn't matter whether I'm doing it. You must do it because I said so!"

This is unhealthy parenting. This is hypocrisy to the max, and it doesn't cut it with our children. They see right through it. Influential parents do not expect their children to live by standards different from those the parents live by. Influential parents expect their children to do as they say *because* the parents are modeling what they are instructing. This is called integrity, and it's a crucial part of influential parenting.

Living by a standard different from what we set for our children—that is, a double standard—is moving *away* from our intended destination, not toward it. If I'm not moving in the direction I want my children to go, I can't be surprised when they aren't moving in that direction either. And if they ever move in a direction I didn't model for them, it will be in spite of me, not because of me.

I'll give you a painful example from our own parenting vault. Kristin and I have an imperfect record when it comes to our adult commitment to church. When we were growing up, church was everything to us. We loved our youth groups. We were the first kids to arrive before service and the last to leave afterward. But two decades marked by painful church experiences as adults left us wounded and dismayed. I served with four churches from my senior year of college until 2014. Three of those experiences were devastating. From 2015 to 2017, Kristin served on staff with two churches—one a great experience and one marred by abusive leadership. Our children became unintended victims of our pain and grief. They loved church, they formed meaningful church relationships even where we had bad experiences, and they were broken-hearted each time things went south.

We loved our last church in the beginning and enthusiastically dove into ministry there. This inner-city church worked with vulnerable people from impoverished areas, a cause that all of us were passionate about. But after a year and a half, things fell apart. Fellow staff members, who were equally passionate about the work, left due to the toxic environment. Eventually, we did too. Both we and our kids were devastated. We felt we no longer had a place in the church.

I want to be clear. We love the church, we believe in the church, and we fully love and follow Jesus. But we have been subjected to some very painful experiences at the hands of the church. We've seen people we love treated horribly for no good reason. And often, the Jesus we saw modeled and heard preached was nothing like the Jesus we see in the Bible. This left us tired and done. We decided to take a break. We are Christ followers, but for a while we just couldn't darken another church door. It was too painful. We didn't want to play any more games. We wanted to be part of a church that lived out the Jesus of the Bible.

In the interim, we intended to conduct family devotions and even invite friends over for home church once a week. But our good intentions weren't backed up by solid direction. We sometimes went weeks without opening the Bible as a family. Biblical practices are important to Kristin and me, but we weren't following through on our values. A few months into this break, we realized our children's attitudes had started to sour, especially toward faith. Kristin and I had found our attitudes growing sour, and our bad attitudes had rubbed off on our children.

We had to face a painful reality, and we had no one to blame but ourselves. We, the adults, weren't modeling what we expected our children to believe and live out. Our good intentions to spiritually influence our children were meaningless without our movement in the right direction. We had to make a serious change because our children weren't buying our weak attempt at leading them in the direction of a strong faith.

Today, we are part of an authentic, loving community of believers near our home with whom we had previously worked. We couldn't be more thankful. Our children's attitudes have revived, and we are growing. But I can't help shuddering when I remember how my directionless intentions endangered my children's spirits.

Intentional Parenting versus Good Intentions

It's important to distinguish between *intentional parenting* and parenting merely with good intentions. Intentional parenting is about purpose, direction, and following through. It's about determining the path we want our family to take and taking it. It's about consistently leading our children with character, values, and integrity. It's about not giving in to BFF or Dreamer parenting or defaulting to a Commander or Instructor mode.

Parenting with nothing more than good intentions is the opposite. Good intentions may celebrate the *idea* of healthy parenting, but they stop short of the action and commitment necessary to turn those ideas into reality.

It bears repeating: we can intend to arrive at a certain destination, but until we actually start moving in that direction, we will never reach that destination. Commit to intentional parenting, not parenting merely with good intentions.

My hope for you is simple. May you determine to be an influential parent in your children's lives. And may you do this by choosing now—whether your children are toddlers or teens—to lead and love with intentionality, direction, and purpose.

Pause to Reflect

1. Are you moving in the direction of your desired destination for your children and your family? Why or why not?

2. Have you been parenting with intentionality or merely with good intentions? Why is this?

3. Take some time to evaluate any possible need to change direction, or simply reaffirm your current direction. What commitment will you make from this moment forward?

17

Worth the Fight

A long time ago, in a galaxy far, far away, I envisioned the way I thought my life would go—my future career, my family, all of it. I had a five-point plan, and nothing was going to stop me. Enter a feisty, young, blue-eyed blonde. I firmly believe that God sent her into my life to wreck all my best plans because truthfully they were quite selfish. My vision left little room for anyone else's plans. I was self-centered and clueless, and I still sometimes struggle in these areas.

One cold November night, Kristin said matter-of-factly that we were going to adopt all our children. I resisted. I couldn't imagine how I could ever love a child I didn't create biologically. Was I wrong!

I wasn't against adoption; I just didn't understand it. My family was created the old-fashioned way (or as a friend once said, "The fun way!"). So I drilled down hard on my plans and stayed the course in my beliefs about my life's direction. Thankfully, Kristin won the battle. Not only did we adopt, but we adopted all our children. All eight. Today, my youngest is eight years old and my oldest (whom we adopted at age twenty-four) is thirty-two. Quite a spread.

I never imagined the story line we are living. But I can tell you from the bottom of my heart that I couldn't have scripted a better story. My best-laid plans and intentions pale in comparison. I feared I couldn't love an adopted child, but now I don't know how a person could not. Even as I type, eight faces flash through my mind, and I love each of them deeper than deep. I would swim the ocean for any of them. They are mine.

I've been to parenting's dark side. I've made more mistakes than I can count. I've failed my children many times. I've had to humble myself and seek their forgiveness. I've succumbed to lecturing, scorning, controlling. And I've tried buddying up, idealizing, and more. These never worked.

When I stopped fighting to win some argument with my children and reset my sights on their hearts instead, everything changed. My love is not based on how they behave or who they are becoming. I see their genius. I see their beautiful spirits. I see into their hearts, and I love what I see. At the end of my life, I would rather know my kids deeply and intimately than have proved some meaningless point of fact. Because it is all worth it.

Their Hearts Are Worth It

The heart inside each of my children is unbelievably worth the right fight. What makes it beat? What makes it glow? What breaks it? What are its wildest dreams? I want to know. I want to spend all the time I can with my amazing children discovering the answers to these questions. And I want to protect and defend what I find in their hearts. When a cold and harsh world tells them they are not good enough, smart enough, pretty enough, cool enough, or talented enough, I want them to know their daddy believes they are, beyond any doubt. I want them to forever know I cherish them.

I don't want to win a single argument or prove a single point if it means I miss any of this. Their hearts are worth too much.

Their Futures Are Worth It

Who will my children become? How will they change the world? What impact will they make on others? How will they defend the vulnerable and deprived? What beautiful mark will they leave?

I want them to know the future is theirs, and that their mom and dad will be here cheering them on, no matter what. I want to reassure them that their mistakes, shortcomings, and failures do not define them and do not determine their future success. I want them to venture into the world fully confident they are loved. And I want them to know our front door is never locked. Home will always be here. Their futures are worth it.

Their Stories Are Worth It

The beautiful, amazing, brilliant, glorious, hilarious, inspiring, motivating story within each of my children is worth the fight. With all I am and have yet to become, I want to champion the story within each one.

I don't understand parents who force their children into the same profession as theirs or impose their choice of college or continually interfere in their friendships or dating relationships. I don't get why parents can't step back, take their hands off, and allow their adult children to follow the path they want to follow or were made to follow. Granted, there are situations in which a parent has to step in if dating or friendship choices aren't healthy and become destructive, but that's the exception, not the rule.

I've long known and admired a particular family. I knew and watched all their children grow up. Their father often said, "This life is theirs to live and become who they want. We celebrate and believe in whatever it is they choose to become. From day one, we've released them into the Lord's hands. They are his." Now there's a concept. Today, all three of he and his wife's children are living healthy, happy, independent lives with their own families here in the United States and abroad. The legacy they began to forge in their children is also being strongly lived out in the lives of their grandchildren.

Championing and supporting our children's unique stories is the only way to raise children who love their lives. I've known many parents who tried to force their plans and wills on their children, only to end up disconnected and estranged. I want to ask, Was it worth it?

I want my children to live the stories they are called to live and want to live. As long as they live lives of character and integrity, I'm behind whatever they choose to become. Their stories are worth it.

Our Family Is Worth It

I will always come home because I love this beautiful, broken, ever-in-repair, hilarious, perfectly imperfect family with which God has blessed me. I don't want to live any other life, even though we've gone through some extremely difficult moments. This is family. It was never meant to look like a magazine cover or a plotline from the Hallmark Channel. If that is what you are waiting for, no wonder you feel discontented or disappointed. Why not cherish what you have, not what you thought you would receive? Your family is worth it.

I fight for the hearts of my children every day. I fight to love them fiercely. I fight to make sure they know every day how cherished and wanted they are. I fight so they know we've always got their backs, we're always cheering for them, and we're always here for them. I fight to defend them against a lonely world that threatens to tear them down and magnify their insecurities. I fight to remind them always how brilliant, beautiful, and amazing they are, even when they feel they are not.

Even when we fight, I fight to win their hearts.

On this journey we call parenting, that's the most important battle to win.

Notes

Chapter 1 Winning the Argument but Losing the Heart

1. Reggie Joiner and Carey Nieuwhof, *Parenting Beyond Your Capacity: Connect Your Family to a Wider Community* (Colorado Springs: David C. Cook, 2010), 100.

2. Joiner and Nieuwhof, *Parenting Beyond Your Capacity*, 100.

Chapter 3 What the Gilmore Girls, Buddy the Elf, General Patton, and Mr. Strickland Share in Common

1. Chrissy Gordon, "Key Findings in Landmark Pornography Study Released," Josh McDowell Ministry, January 19, 2016, https://www.josh.org/key-findings-in-landmark-pornography-study-released.

2. Mike Berry, "Parenting on Purpose Part 2—Creating Boundaries for Your Children (podcast)," *Confessions of an Adoptive Parent* (blog), June 2, 2016, https://confessionsofanadoptiveparent.com/parenting-on-purpose-part-2-creating-boundaries-for-your-children-podcast.

Chapter 4 The Ugly Stepsisters of Parenting

1. "Politik," Coldplay, track 1 on *A Rush of Blood to the Head*, recorded 2001–2, Capitol Records.

Chapter 6 Fourth Place Can Win

1. Carl E. Pickhardt, "Adolescence and the Influence of Parents," *Psychology Today*, October 18, 2010, https://www.psychologytoday.com/us/blog/surviving-your-childs-adolescence/201010/adolescence-and-the-influence-parents.

2. Pickhardt, "Adolescence and the Influence of Parents."

Chapter 7 You Need a Bigger Circle

1. Joiner and Nieuwhof, *Parenting Beyond Your Capacity*, 62.
2. Joiner and Nieuwhof, *Parenting Beyond Your Capacity*, 63.

Chapter 8 Time Is Not on Your Side

1. Joiner and Nieuwhof, *Parenting Beyond Your Capacity*, 135.
2. "Social Media—Statistics and Facts," Statista, accessed April 18, 2018, https://www.statista.com/topics/1164/social-networks.
3. "Number of Monthly Active Instagram Users from January 2013 to June 2018," Statista, accessed July 2018, https://www.statista.com/statistics/253577/number-of-monthly-active-instagram-users.
4. "Most Famous Social Network Sites Worldwide as of July 2018, Ranked by Number of Active Users," Statista, accessed August 2018, https://www.statista.com/statistics/272014/global-social-networks-ranked-by-number-of-users.
5. Linda Blake and Ben Worthen, "Distracted: Texting While Parenting," *Wall Street Journal*, September 28, 2012, video, 5:48, https://www.wsj.com/video/distracted-texting-while-parenting/36646FB6-F606-4ED1-8CF1-02CDCDA5F772.html.

Chapter 9 Be Fully There

1. Jen Hatmaker (@jenhatmaker), "Having Coffee with This Son," Instagram photo, March 10, 2018, https://www.instagram.com/p/BgJaUmgBnjO/?utm_source=ig_web_copy_link.

Chapter 10 I Would Rather Be the Tortoise

1. *Mr. and Mrs. Smith*, directed by Doug Liman (Los Angeles: Regency Enterprises, 2005).

Chapter 12 A Parent's Greatest Enemy

1. *Meet the Robinsons*, directed by Stephen Anderson (Burbank, CA: Walt Disney Pictures, 2007).

Chapter 13 Potato Salad and Headstones

1. *Dead Poets Society*, directed by Peter Weir (Burbank, CA: Buena Vista Pictures, 1989).

Chapter 16 Direction Determines Destination

1. Andy Stanley, *The Principle of the Path: How to Get from Where You Are to Where You Want to Be* (Nashville: Thomas Nelson, 2008), 14.
2. John Harrington and Cheyenne Buckingham, "Broken Hearts: A Rundown of the Divorce Capital of Every State," *USA Today*, February 2, 2018, https://www.usatoday.com/story/money/economy/2018/02/02/broken-hearts-rundown-divorce-capital-every-state/1078353001/.

Mike Berry is the cofounder, along with his wife, Kristin, of the award-winning parenting blog *Confessions of an Adoptive Parent* and the virtual support and resource site for foster and adoptive parents, Oasis Community. He is a featured writer and influencer for the Disney website Babble.com, and his work has also been featured on *Yahoo Parenting*, The Good Men Project, *The Huffington Post*, RightNow Media, Michael Hyatt's Platform University, and goinswriter.com. A sought-after speaker, Mike travels extensively throughout the year to camps, retreats, and conferences across the United States. Before becoming a full-time author and speaker, he spent seventeen years in family-life ministry in churches in Ohio and Indiana. He lives on a farm just north of Indianapolis, Indiana, with his wife and their eight children.

CONNECT WITH **MIKE BERRY** AT

CONFESSIONSOFANADOPTIVEPARENT.COM

MIKE@CONFESSIONSMAIL.COM

 @confessionsofanadoptiveparent   @itsmikeberry

 @confessionsofaparent

Connect with

BakerBooks

Relevant. Intelligent. Engaging.

Sign up for announcements about
new and upcoming titles at

www.bakerbooks.com/signup

f ReadBakerBooks

🐦 ReadBakerBooks